REACHING OUT TO THE POOR

Also published by Macmillan

By Geeta Somjee

NARROWING THE GENDER GAP

By A. H. Somjee

DEMOCRATIC PROCESS IN A DEVELOPING SOCIETY

PARALLELS AND ACTUALS OF POLITICAL DEVELOPMENT

POLITICAL CAPACITY IN DEVELOPING SOCIETIES

POLITICAL SOCIETY IN DEVELOPING COUNTRIES

Reaching out to the Poor

The Unfinished Rural Revolution

Geeta Somjee

and

A. H. Somjee

MACMILLAN

First published 1989

Published by
THE MACMILLAN PRESS LTD
Houndmills, Basingstoke, Hampshire RG21 2XS
and London
Companies and representatives
throughout the world

Typeset by TecSet Ltd, Wallington, Surrey

British Library Cataloguing in Publication Data
Somjee, Geeta, 1930–
Reaching out to the poor.
1. (Republic) India. (Republic) Western
India. Dairy cooperatives. Social aspects
I. Title   II. Somjee, A. H., 1925–
306'344
ISBN 0–333–46784–1   hardcover
ISBN 0–333–46794–9   paperback

To the farmers, veterinarians, dairy technologists and socially concerned individuals of
Gujarat who, together, made an effort to zero
in on rural poverty

Contents

Preface

This book is about the poor and the constraints of social and economic relationships within which they are trapped. It is also about their inability, given such constraints, to escape from poverty all by themselves. In their case neither the provisions of public policy nor specific development stimulus are enough to help them. They need socially concerned individuals, who can mobilize them, and economic organizations which can specifically target them for development. The extent of the effectiveness of such individuals and organizations would depend on their realistic understanding of the complexity of cultural, economic, political and human factors which condemn the poor not only to economic deprivation but also to a many-sided incapacity to be able to fight back on their own. As such this book concentrates on the poor, and the complex nature of their limitations, rather than on abstract notions of poverty.

In different societies the poor are poor for different reasons. Not all those reasons are purely economic. Explanations of the conditions of the poor only in terms of their economic deprivation often fail to take into account the wider cultural, political and human problems which go hand in hand with poverty. Such a broad approach becomes all the more necessary for countries where poverty is sought to be justified by means of references to social organization, culture and a deeply internalized belief that the poor are poor not because some have more than their fair share but because the makers of us all so ordained. Village after village in rural India disowns responsibility for the less fortunate among them and echoes the deadly conviction that 'there always will be poor'. And if there is someone who can do something for them, they maintain, it is either the *sarkar* (government) or some development agency from outside.

Neither the sarkar nor the bulk of development agencies have had any appreciable measure of success in fighting poverty. However, among the economic organizations functioning in rural areas, those which sprang up by means of grass-roots efforts, and were sustained by such efforts, have had some measure of success. The milk cooperatives of western India, with a grass-roots base and with one weapon at their disposal, namely, dairying, came face to face with the resourceless poor of their respective districts. And despite the fact that officially those organizations were supposed to be concerned with 'milk producers' only, a number of their veterinary personnel and technocrats, without specifically formulated policies, got involved, often on their own, in efforts to induct the non-producers from the poorer strata of rural communities into milk cooperatives. Much of their effort was the product of what they felt needed doing. Some of them succeeded in convincing their superiors of the need to broaden the scope of their organizations, others did not. Wherever such socially concerned personnel succeeded in getting the support of their superiors, the results were impressive. In others there was much to be desired. In this book we shall examine the uneven performance, in that respect, of the four milk cooperatives of western India, namely Amul, Dudhsagar, Sumul and Sabar.

As we shall see in detail in the following pages, Dudhsagar, in Mehsana district, probably by now one of the greatest milk cooperatives in the country, has over 14 per cent of its membership from among the landless farmers. And although some of those landless have access to others' farms, either as relatives or as sharecroppers, a large proportion in this category also consists of the landless labourers. Given the extraordinary dedication of its veterinary personnel and senior executives to the cause of the poor, chances are that within the foreseeable future the membership proportion of its landless may go still higher.

Similarly, Sumul dairy, in Surat district, succeeded in turning its *Adivasis* (tribals) – who had neither the culture of drinking milk nor of maintaining milch animals worth the name – into milk producers to produce milk. More than seventy per cent of its milk is now collected from its Adivasi villages. Such a double revolution, human and economic, was brought about by its dedicated veterinary personnel.

A similar move was afoot in Sabar dairy, in Sabarkantha district, where this youngest of the four dairies was getting deeply involved in the district's poor, again through its veterinary personnel. And since its top executive himself was deeply involved in what his junior colleagues were doing, Sabar was able to penetrate nearly one-fourth of its tribal villages in the shortest possible time.

Finally, Amul, India's premier milk cooperative. Although it had generated an enormous liquidity through the sale of milk (Rs1610m in 1989), and thereby helped the district to improve its agriculture, stimulated its industrial development of medium-scale industries, of very high quality, in various small towns including Anand, and helped build major markets for the sale of grains, vegetables, agricultural implements, auto parts, etc., its concentration on the poor of the district, in relative terms, has been less impressive. What it has done in recent years, however, is to reach out to its poor by means of its specially designed health service.

Despite such impressive performance from the four milk cooperatives, their ability to reach out to their poor was very limited indeed. The unreached poor in those districts far outnumbered those that had been reached. And no one was more aware of that than the vets, technocrats and extension workers who had come face to face with the rural poor. At the same time, however, as we shall see in the following pages, these cooperatives were also, in relative terms, the most efficient agencies working in rural India. And that was due, in a large measure, to the nature of their economic organizations and the social concern of their personnel.

But what is of greater significance to us here is the baffling nature of their problem. As those organizations and individuals shifted their attention from abstract notions of poverty to the actual poor, they began to realize that the problem that they were faced with had many sides to it. Of these the economic needs received the maximum attention and the others went unnoticed. The four case studies here, based on our longitudinal field research, give us a glimpse into the complex world of the constraints of the poor. Those constraints, as we shall see in this volume, stunted the social and political capacity of the poor to such an extent that they were unable to derive benefits from the new economic opportunities created for them. In a situation of antecedent social inequality there was bound to be a differentiated response to development stimulus. However, within the same situation even those development measures which were specially meant for the poor either did not reach them or could evoke, at best, minimal response. Their response, nevertheless, remarkably improved when socially concerned individuals, who believed in their development through their own self-involvement, lent an initial helping hand. The response of the same group to development opportunity did not go very far when social workers practised development paternalism of one form or another. We hope to be able to examine a variety of such development stimulus–response cases in a number of rural communities in the four districts to be able to identify the extent of their effectiveness.

In response to the establishment of various milk cooperatives, a kind of social queue was formed in various rural communities whereby the individuals who were already better off were the first to derive benefit from such a new economic opportunity. But such a segment of rural society gradually reduced its interest in dairying because of a more attractive economic alternative in various kinds of cash crops which the increasing availability of water, fertilizer and improved seeds had made possible.

As the interest of such a segment of the dairy community began to decline, its place was taken up by agriculturist castes, traditionally close to it. Such a shift led to competition for political power among the agriculturist castes, around the milk cooperatives of various rural communities, and also to an ethnic reshuffle for social status. The new economic institution of dairying also provided an opportunity to the lower castes, tribals, and *Harijans* (ex-untouchables) provided they had milch animals.

But such a penetration of the milk coops in various rural communities, from top-down on the traditional social scale, could not get past, at least in the initial years, those who could not be classified as 'milk producers'. Such a group constituted, roughly, more than one-third of the rural community and a much larger percentage of the poor.

Over the years, through the improvement in water facilities for agriculture, making farm cuttings available to the landless labourers as a part of their nominal wages, six to nine months in a year, government subsidies and loans for buying milch animals, and in some cases the establishment of cooperative fodder farms, a segment of the poor, who were also landless, were brought within the cooperative dairies. Behind that there were the tireless efforts of the vets, procurement officers, extension personnel and technocrats. Such efforts also began changing, gradually, the nature of cooperative dairies from their earlier emphasis on productivity to reaching out to those who were left out of its economic and social enterprise.

An analysis of the economic background of the membership of the four milk cooperatives suggests that they have increasingly become the organizations of the small, marginal and landless farmers. What is more, the landless farmers within their membership, some with access to land, have also become one of the largest groups. The figures in Table 1 give us an indication of such a shift.

The figures suggest that 67.96 per cent of Dudhsagar, 76.90 per cent of Amul, 76.02 percent of Sumul, and 69.09 per cent of Sabar Dairy membership now consists of landless, marginal and small farmers. The milk cooperatives of Gujarat have thus come a long way from their earlier membership when medium and large farmers, generally from higher castes, predominated in them. What is more, in two out of four of those dairies, the landless farmers, with some

TABLE 1   *Landownership status of the four dairies*[1]

Amul Dairy: Landownership Background of Members (1984)

Landless Farmers	27%
Marginal Farmers	16.4%
Small Farmers	33.5%
Others	23.1%

Dhudhsagar Dairy: Landownership Background of Members (1986)

Landless Farmers	13.54%
Marginal Farmers	26.28%
Small Farmers	28.14%
Others	32.04%

Sumul Dairy: Landownership Background of Members (1987)

Landless Farmers	36.38%
Marginal Farmers	21.79%
Small Farmers	17.85%
Others	23.98%

Sabar Dairy: Landownership Background of Members (1986)

Landless Farmers	15.86%
Marginal Farmers	26.14%
Small Farmers	27.10%
The Rest	30.90%

---

among them having access to land, constitute more than a quarter to more than one-third of their total membership. That indeed was a remarkable achievement for those organizations which have been continually trying to penetrate the poorer segments of rural communities.[2]

Our longitudinal field research in those four districts was spread over two decades. In December 1960, when we were faculty at the M.S. University of Baroda, Tribhuvandas Patel, one of the founding fathers of Amul Dairy, invited us to have a look at the village called Asodar, in Kaira District, with a view to finding out the changes that were taking place in it as a result of its newly started milk cooperative. Since then we have visited the same and several other villages in the four districts several times, updating our findings and making sure of the validity of our inferences drawn from our observations. The greatest difficulty we faced in this kind of research was when to draw a line. Tentatively we drew such a line a couple of times only to find in our following visits that the rural communities we were looking at had registered additional changes with marked significance for our work on social change generally. While the economic performance of those communities was registering a slower pace of change, socially and politically they were stirring up all the time. But such stirrings, we subsequently realized, had still a long way to go before they could begin altering, significantly, the nature of economic relationships themselves.

Our selection of various rural communities in the four districts was guided by consideration of the various dimensions involved in understanding the complexity of any effort at reaching out to the poor. Towards such an understanding we had taken into account economic, cultural, ethnic, political and developmental dimensions and then sought to identify and explain what in fact had helped or hindered the advancement of the poor, all that with reference to the new economic opportunity provided by the milk cooperatives.

In trying to do that we had adopted a contextual approach. We believe that it is pointless to talk about the poor out of the economic, cultural, political and human contexts which have contributed to their being poor in the first place.

As stated earlier, we had focused our attention on the poor and not on abstract notions of poverty. Such notions, we believe, often remain indifferent to the many-sided reasons of poverty. On the other hand, if we concentrate on who the poor in specific communities actually are, and what, in actual practice, frustrates their effort to improve their economic condition, we are more likely to get a realistic answer. Such a search would then take us to a lot of related areas which encompass the world of the poor, but also beyond the narrow confines of academic specializations.

In our field research, spread over a long period, far more individuals were helpful to us than we can possibly mention or even remember. Among others we want to thank the founding fathers and chief executives of the four milk cooperatives, vets, procurement and extension officers, chairmen and secretaries of various village cooperatives, all of whom were willing to answer our searching questions, patiently, year after year. We owe a special debt of gratitude to Tribhuvandas Patel, Dr V. Kurien, Natwarlal Dave, Bhagwandas

Bandukwala, H. M. Dalaya, V. H. Shah, Dr A. Chothani, Dr Uma Vyas,Prafullabhai Bhatt, Narendrabahi Patel, Dr S. N. Patel and Dr Kodagali, all of these were at one time or another connected with Amul. We also wish to express our gratitude for help in understanding the social and economic life of the district made possible by means of discussions with the late Bhailalbahi Patel, H. M. Patel, Manibhai Ashabhai Patel, Vitthalbhai Patel, Shivabhai Patel, Sammy Mistry, Kanubhai Patel, Ramanbhai Prajapati, and Ranchhodbhai Solanki. We also wish to thank Motibhai Chaudhury, B. C. Bhatt, and Dr A. S. Dave of Dhudhsagar. Our understanding of the district of Mehsana and its peculiar problems was made possible by means of discussions with Karsanbhai Chaudhury of Boratwada, the late Rambhai Chaudhury of Pamol and the late Shambhubhai Naik of Dudhsagar. We also owe a debt of gratitude to Daskaka, Dr Thakorebhai Patel, Dr H. A. Ghasia and Dr Gupta of Sumul. Our thanks are also due to Bhurabhai Patel, Babubhai Rabari, Dr Haribhai Patel, Dr P. S. Soni, and Mr Ishwarbhai Patel of Sabar.

Our repeated field visits to the villages of Gujarat were made possible by research grants from the Social Sciences and Humanities Research Council of Canada. The years when we could not find such grants, we went on our own.

We also wish to express our thanks to the editors of *Economic Development and Cultural Change*, the *Journal of Asian and African Studies* and the *Journal of Developing Studies* for their kind permission to include some parts of our papers which we published in those journals earlier.

In a work of this nature there are bound to be many shortcomings. For whatever are there in this volume, we alone are responsible.

West Vancouver

Geeta Somjee
A. H. Somjee

1 Amul Dairy: the foundation

Amul designed the framework within which the cooperative dairy movement in India evolved. It thus built not only the structure of 'cooperative' for the dairy movement, but also made it highly pragmatic for its adaptation in other parts of India and in developing countries in general. With its enormous success also came a few problems, both foreseen and unforeseen. Some of these were due to a partial loss of its early élan and a declining commitment to pursue, doggedly, the intractable problem of rural poverty with the help of the one single weapon at its disposal, namely cooperative dairying. Nevertheless, what it did achieve, and is still struggling to achieve, in rural areas will go down in history as one of the greatest triumphs of post-independence India. Its achievements and limitations also furnish us with an insight into all that is possible, and difficult, in reaching out to the poor in a developing society.

We shall analyse these and other related themes under the following headings: the beginnings; the changing composition of Amul's milk producers; some rural communities; interdependence of technocrats and politicians; and some general observations. We shall now examine each of these points in some detail.

THE BEGINNINGS

Amul has been an offshoot of the Indian national movement. In its establishment and development major national figures such as Sardar Patel and Morarji Desai were involved. The groundwork for cooperative organization, which was meant to protect the average milk producer at the village level from ruthless milk traders, was laid by nationalist leaders, and even when the technologists subsequently joined it, its philosophy, direction and organization continued to be what its founding fathers gave it. Its technologists, while building, operating and replicating similar organizations elsewhere in India, never lost sight of the social concerns of its founding fathers for protecting the rural poor. They worked with politicians of the post-independence era, who were several cuts below the nationalist

1

leaders in their integrity and social concerns, and brought to bear the fruits of their ability to build and efficiently run complex organizations connecting a large number of rural communities in the district. They introduced the modern technology of dairying and the science of cattle improvement, and, above all, launched effective marketing techniques so as to secure maximum, and assured, return for the average milk producer. Without them and their organizational effort the average milk producer at the village level would have been defenceless.

The fact that the milk cooperative movement developed in Kaira district was significant. The district has had, for a long time, surplus milk which in the past was turned into *ghee* (purified butter) and shipped outside. The town of Mahemdabad was in the past a flourishing centre of the ghee trade, and traders from Ahmedabad and Bombay regularly bought their supplies from it.

The nature of the trade in milk and milk products began to change when a businessman from the village of Nar brought from Bombay an imported cream separator. Later on similar machines, with all their crudities, were locally made. The cream separator changed the nature of the milk trade in the district. It also adversely affected the flourishing ghee trade in the region.

The British army needed a steady supply of milk and milk products, which in turn created a need for the rationalization of the milk business. Such an effort gave rise to a new breed of middlemen in the milk business who sought official protection and the exclusive right to receive milk from producers.

In order to ensure a steady supply of milk and milk products, a government-run central creamery was established in the city of Bombay. After that more creameries were created in the milk surplus district of Kaira to make sure that the Bombay government creamery and its dependent British army did not go without milk or milk products.

The intervention on the part of government in the milk business created a flourishing class of milk traders and milk product manufacturers. Such a class was known in the district as the *sanchawallas* (those who operated machines). They dictated the price of milk, and the farmer, who had no other recourse, had to accept it. After separating the cream from milk, the sanchawallas used to throw away the residue in village streets leaving behind a dried trail of white liquid in one rural community after another. The mode of production based on cream separators thus wasted all other properties of milk except fat. And to that extent, in what was a monopoly situation, the producers got very little in return for what they offered. An Englishman from Warwickshire, by the name of Reeves, who ran his own milk dairy in the town of Nadiad, appropriately called this period in dairy industry 'an era of waste'.

Soon another wave of technological development hit the milk industry. This time it was directed towards the ingredient left out in the fatless milk, namely casein. In 1911, a German technologist called Koehler was invited to a village called Samarkha by an enterprising silk merchant to set up an industrial unit to extract casein. A Parsi gentleman called Banker also joined them. Initially Koehler got the fatless milk free of charge, but when he started extracting casein from it, the price went up. Consequently, Koehler made an arrangement to receive whole milk so that he could get both cream and casein out of it. Such an arrangement from his point of view was much more economical. The milk traders who supplied him with milk were known as the Doshi brothers.

Koehler kept the simple technology of casein-making strictly to himself. He regularly mixed some kind of an unknown chemical with milk but would not tell anyone what it was. Moreover, he made all his employees sign an undertaking that they would not start rival casein-making factories of their own. While his employees knew the mechanical, and to some extent the chemical, process involved, they did not know what kind of secret chemical Koehler mixed towards the end of the process to get casein. For the purposes of mixing the mysterious chemical, he had trained a special assistant called Mansukhlal Kapasi. But Kapasi was not as trustworthy as Keohler had thought him to be. In Koehler's absence, he once deliberately refrained from mixing the mysterious chemical and still casein came out at the other end of the manufacturing process. Kapasi was now convinced that Koehler, the great German technologist, had fooled everyone. What Koehler had in fact used was water with a slightly misleading smell of a chemical.

After that, Kapasi approached various firms to which Koehler supplied casein and quoted a much lower price for it. When Koehler came to know about it, he went after Kapasi with his gun, shot at him but missed. Later on Koehler filed a suit against Kapasi and the latter was sentenced to two months' imprisonment for the breach of his undertaking. The higher court, however, reversed the decision. And thus ended the cloak-and-dagger phase of technology in the Indian milk industry.

Later on Kapasi started his own creamery and casein manufacturing company at Anand. With the declaration of the First World War, Koehler was locked up as an enemy alien. His partners, however, continued his business. Since there were too many casein makers in the district, Keohler's firm could not stand the competition and finally folded up.

During that period there came yet another industrial entrepreneur in the milk industry, namely Pestonji Polson, the maker of the famous Polson butter. He modernized the milk industry by making use of imported up-to-date machinery. He too owed his rise to the shortage of dairy products in the dining rooms of the British army. An army officer in charge of food supplies, namely Colonel Dickson, persuaded Pestonji Polson to set up a mechanized unit at Anand so that the army might get an uninterrupted supply of butter.

Before entering into the butter-making business, Pestonji Edulji Dalal, later on known as Pestonji Polson, used to sell, in Bombay's Crowford market, what he called 'French coffee', which was a blend of coffee and chicory. The armed forces needed coffee in large quantities and Pestonji was therefore able to do a roaring business for himself. His coffee business brought him in close contact with Colonel Dickson and other officers who gave him the nickname of 'Polly'. When he hit the big time, as a supplier of coffee and later on butter, those army officials persuaded him to change his name to Pestonji Polson,and give himself the brand name, and the respectability, of a western sounding name such as 'Polson'. Thus was born a respectable trade name, which became a household word for the Indian middle class for the following three decades.

The highly mechanized dairy at Anand started functioning in 1929, and during the following decade Polson vastly increased his production of cream, butter and casein, and some of his products were exported to the countries of south-east Asia and Africa. In 1934, Polson established a pasteurization plant at Anand, which was the only one of its kind in the east. And he appropriately named his organization the Polson Model Dairy.

The outbreak of the Second World War in 1939 once again boosted Polson's fortunes, and during that period his production of butter reached a record high of three million pounds in weight a year. But the benefits of this did not reach the farmers. And given the monopoly situation they did not even have recourse to an alternative market. As late as 1945 there was no relaxation of the monopoly. The then government of Bombay, which also included the administration of Kaira district, produced a milk scheme of its own which banned the export of milk and milk products outside the district. That gave a continued advantage to Polson. For the farmers of the district that was the last straw. They were hoping that with the end of the war the situation would improve, but it did not. They therefore started turning to the nationalist leaders for help.

Sardar Patel, the towering nationalist leader, who came from the village Karamsad, which is hardly five miles from Anand, had been toying with the idea of a milk cooperative since 1942, but since he was far too immersed in the national movement itself, he could not pay enough attention to it. Moreover, during the same year he was imprisoned, when the Quit India Movement was launched, and was finally released in 1945.

The Polson dairy, apart from farmers' resentment of it, brought out the ire of the average nationalist-minded citizen during the war years. For one thing it was too closely associated with the *raj*. It therefore became a target of a much wider agitation.

In 1946, when the chances of Indian independence did not look very bright, Sardar Patel, recently released from prison, and his associates such as Morarji Desai and Tribhuvandas Patel (TK), together with several other political workers, organized what came to be known as 'the Satyagraha of the Fourteen Villages'. They launched their highly effective non-cooperation movement by not selling milk to Polson. During the agitation some of the farmers and district level leaders were arrested. By that time the government of Bombay also realized that it could not go on with continued favours to Polson. It therefore agreed to the demand of the agitators for a milk cooperative organization of their own. On December 14, 1946, a milk cooperative known as Anand Milk Union Ltd., abbreviated as AMUL, came into existence. It was destined to become one of the greatest and the most prestigious farmer-owned milk cooperative societies in the world.

The fact that Amul was so closely associated with the topmost nationalist leaders of India, at the very height of the freedom movement, gave assurance to the farmers of a fair deal for them in the new organization. They were therefore willing to give the new organization a try. The farmers of Kaira, as we shall see in the following pages, built their own grass-roots movement to establish, operate and effectively protect their own interests through it. This

they did under the guidance of political workers as well as technocrats. So then the three principal makers of Amul were the
farmers, political workers, and technocrats.[1]

In the four decades after its establishment, Amul, both in terms of
participation by milk producers and milk productivity itself, expanded phenomenally. The following figures will give us some idea
of it:

TABLE 2   *Growth of Amul, 1947–86*

Year	Number of village milk cooperatives	Number of milk producers who became members
1947–48	8	432
1956–57	107	26,759
1971–72	744	215,000
1985–86	872	365,000

Amul kept itself closely in touch with the principal political figures of
Indian society. In 1955, when Jawaharlal Nehru visited it, it produced
1,600,000 litres of milk per day. And three decades later, when his
grandson, Rajiv Gandhi, visited it, Amul's milk collection had risen
to a whopping 1 m litres of milk per day at the height of season. Its
sale of milk and milk products brought into the district Rs1610m
(1989). That was indeed a phenomenal achievement.[2]

THE CHANGING COMPOSITION OF AMUL'S MILK
PRODUCERS

Let us now briefly examine the changing composition of Amul's milk
producing community. In 1984 the organizers of Amul maintained
that its milk producing community was largely drawn from small
farmers. It claimed that 77 per cent of its total membership of 365,000
members consisted of milk producers who were small farmers,
marginal farmers and landless farmers. The total figures were as
follows:

TABLE 3   *Numbers and types of farmers in Amul (1984)*[3]

Landless farmers who were members of coop	112,418 (27%)
Small farmers who were members of coop	139,558 (33.5%)
Marginal farmers who were members of coop	68,279 (16.4%)
Big farmers who were members of coop	49,243 (11.7%)
Others (farmers with more than one household)	42,243 (11.4%)

Over the four decades since Amul's inception the composition of its membership, both in terms of ethnicity and landholding, had significantly changed. Amul's earlier membership was largely drawn from individuals who were small, medium and large landholders. This was true of the bulk of villages where the Patidars were either in a majority or at the forefront of their public life. In such villages Patidars were also, in a real sense, the founding fathers of most of their village milk cooperatives.

It was because of their initiative-taking disposition, search for increased income and profit and willingness to join the farmers' strike in 1946 that TK, Morarji Desai and Sardar Patel were able to shake off the stranglehold of the Polson dairy, the milk contractors and the milk bureaucracy.

A number of Patidars were thus the veterans of the pre-independence struggle for building new economic institutions which benefited the people. But they were also the first, and the principal, set of beneficiaries of the newly created economic opportunities. In a sense they had far too many historical experiences which had given them a special advantage, vis-à-vis other ethnic groups, in making use of those opportunities.

As a landed community, they had the experience of being a part of the revenue bureaucracy during the Mughal and, later on, British period. After independence, their numerical limitations had given them certain electoral setbacks in competitive politics for public office. They, nevertheless, had continued to enjoy advantages of their awareness of the laws governing land, contact with administrative officials and politicians, urban links, confidence which came out of their belonging to a relatively higher caste, and, above all, economic power.

All these favourable factors no doubt gave to the Patidars an advantage in developing a dairy industry and in keeping a firm hold on village coops where they could overcome their numerical disadvantage by means of building a support structure from among other ethnic groups. However, their interest in dairying began to flag when they discovered the scope for greater returns from agriculture. As returns from agriculture, and particularly from cash crops and vegetables, increased, the Patidars of various villages started paying much less attention to dairying. In relative terms what an income from the sale of buffalo milk could add was not very appealing to most of them. That attitude, however, began to change when cross-bred cows, with the possibility of engaging in dairying on a large-scale commercial basis, hit the scene in late 1970s and early 1980s.

But most Patidars, particularly in Kaira, had already economically diversified themselves too much to return to cross-bred cow dairying in a big way. The increased liquidity from agricultural income, including milk, had helped a part of their families to start commercial and then industrial ventures, in some cases, in nearby towns. The bulk of commercial and industrial entrepreneurships in and around towns such as Anand, Nadiad, Cambay and even Ahemdabad were by Patidars whose agricultural base had helped them to move on to the next stage of their economic advancement.

In the meanwhile, even before the Patidars were losing interest in dairying, other ethnic groups in the social queue, as it were, were entering it. For such groups, given their own economic limitations, a supplementary income from dairying was indeed a great help. The ethnic groups which came up the dairying ladder, as we shall see, were those of the Kshatriyas and Venkars (weavers – Harijans), the latter being way down in traditional social hierarchy.

Contrary to the popular belief, the Patidars with all their high visibility, articulateness to the point of garrulity, and social and economic prominence, were less than one-fifth of the district's population. Various estimates put their numbers from 14 to 17 per cent of Kaira's population.

Contrary also to a lot of generalizations about their control and domination of the public institutions of the district, including the village milk cooperatives, the Patidars controlled less than half of them. In August 1986, out of 856 milk cooperatives affiliated to Amul, Patidars were chairmen of 313. The Kshatriyas controlled 449, Muslims 36, Venkars (ex-untouchables) 5, and other castes the remainder.

There were also examples of villages with an overwhelming Kshatriya population, and milk cooperative membership, going in search of the most efficient managers which they believed to be the Patidars. Later on we shall illustrate this by referring to the village of Asodar, which for years elected the same Patidar as its milk coop chairman when the membership of its executive committee was overwhelmingly Kshatriya and the local Panchayat was also continuously controlled by them.

The heartland of Patidar is locally known as Charotar. It consists of the regions covered by the Anand, Nadiad, and Petlad *talukas* (sub-districts). Charotar is a region which produced many dynamic leaders such as Sardar Patel, H. M. Patel, TK, Bhailalbhai Patel, Babubhai Jashbhai Patel, Nanubahi Amin, Vitthalbahi Patel, C. S. Patel, Manibhai Ashabhai Patel, I. G. Patel (the director of the London School of Economics in 1986), engineers, laser scientists, brilliant physicians, and a large number of high achievers in social, economic and educational fields. But even in that region, only in twelve villages do the Patidars have a numerical majority. In the rest the Kshatriyas outnumber the Patidars, and in a number of cases dominate their public institutions.

The Kshatriyas, in relative terms, have been far more cohesive than the highly individualistic Patidars. In the past the cleavages among the Kshatriyas often ran on the lines of the various sub-ethnic groups among them. But such cleavages began to be bridged ever since Madhavsingh Solanki rose to political prominence in the politics of Gujarat.

Such a closing of ranks took a lot of effort. Since Kshatriyas are nearly half of the district's population, they became the target of electioneering politicians in search of en bloc voting. Towards that purpose, the Swatantra Party encouraged the persistence of Kshatriya Sabha and the Congress, in order to divide the former's advantage, established a rival organisation called Kshatriya Samaj. Both those organisations were controlled by feudal Rajput elements with the help of the district's Patidar leaders in both the parties. Such organizations, however, could not deliver the political results because of the split. Because of the presence of two rival bodies, the Kshatriya political cleavage split villages and neighbourhoods throughout the district and could not cash in on its numerical strength.

What finally brought them together was the hope of putting one of their own men, not a feudal Rajput, in the office of the Chief Minister of Gujarat. Such a possibility electrified them and roused their hope for economic advancement. In his six years' term of office,

Madhavsingh Solanki promised them much but actually delivered very little. By the time he was forced out of office in 1985, the inter-ethnic relations within various public institutions, including the milk cooperatives, were at their lowest.

The stress on the inter-ethnic relationships helped neither the Patidars nor the Kshatriyas. For one thing the bulk of Patidars are not big landholders. In fact their landholding is not very much bigger than a large number of Kshatriyas. Once we move away from the large landholding Patidars, who have a record of exploitation of the village poor, the economic strength of the Patidars is very much a product of hard work, education, economic drive and of resourcefulness generally, rather than of the size of their land. Through their resourcefulness they also get much more out of land. Such a performance, although it becomes an object of envy of the Kshatriyas, also helps the latter to look for certain standards of possible economic achievement.

In the social and ethnic queue, which formed in the district, the Kshatriyas began getting into dairying as Patidar interest in it began to flag. The bulk of the membership of the district's milk coop is now Kshatriya. But that is as far as the numbers go. However, in terms of sheer skill in maintaining and breeding animals, and getting more out of their bovine investment, the Kshatriyas have a long way to go.

Although the Kshatriyas of Kaira, unlike the Patidars, have yet to hit the wider economic scene of the district, they certainly have begun to supplement their income by means of dairying. Since an overwhelming number of Kshatriyas are small and marginal farmers, the supplementary income from milk is far more important to them than to the Patidars who get much more by way of their agricultural income, with greater skill and choice of crops.

The two entrepreneurs among the Kshatriyas, namely, Babubhai Mathurbhai Chavada and Ranchhodbhai Solanki, both located in the town of Anand, followed the pattern of Patidar economic progression, from agriculture to commerce, by diversifying the financial and human resources of the family. But such commercial progression is also possible in the field of dairy products.

The Kshatriyas of the district thus have to go beyond dairying and dairy products in their economic drive. Given the ethnic tension which crystallized during the Madhavsingh regime, the Kshatriyas may have a much bigger clientele from among their fellow ethnics provided they go beyond dairying and also remain competitive.

With all their long-drawn conflicts with the Patidars, over land, public office and social status, the Kshatriyas are also in an emulative relationship with them. Their agricultural income, supplemented by income from dairying, should have prepared them to move into towns with diversified commercial enterprises. But they did not. What stood in the way was their traditional practice of waiting for *sarkar* or asking ethnic leaders above them to tell them what they should do next. In that respect their entrepreneurial capability is still in the process of development. But so far they have not followed that route. Along with Muslims, Adivasis and Harijans, at least in Gujarat, they have remained too closely associated with the government of the day. In continuing to depend on the *sarkar* they held themselves back from emulating the Patidars and from putting to further economic use the additional liquidity which dairying in the district has provided to them.

This then brings us to the socially and economically lower groups in the district, including the Harijans, who could or could not join the growing number of milk producers in the district.

The cooperative organization of Amul was established in 1946 so as to help the 'poor' of the district. The then 'poor' of the district, by definition, were the farmers per se who were also milk producers but were not allowed to market it wherever they wanted to. The villains of that period were the milk contractors, the agents of the Polson dairy, and, above all, the milk bureaucracy, including the Milk Commissioner. By logical inference, therefore, the poor and the exploited were the farmers who produced milk regardless of the size of their landholding and sources of agricultural income.

Such a perception on the part of Amul began to change when it launched a drive for a bigger membership of milk cooperatives, wherever milk cooperatives were already established, and for the establishment of new ones in those villages of the district which did not have such an organization. Such a drive, initially, was confined to farmers with *sadhan* or the means for dairying, i.e. land and a milch animal.

As the demand for milk increased the question was whether it could produce new milk producers to supply more milk to it. That meant equipping the resourceless with the resources for dairying. While it could not tackle the problem of land, what it could do, nevertheless, was to see if those without land could be brought into the category of the new milk producers of the district. Earlier, to

Amul, to think in terms of transforming the landless into milk producers was a contradiction in terms.

Among the landless farmers, who were still out of the milk producing community, there was a variety of ethnic groups. And then some among them, in particular the Harijans, had an added disadvantage. Earlier, the organizers of Amul had to threaten with closure those village milk coops which refused to accept milk from Harijans or made them stand in a separate queue. Such Harijans had the *sadhan*, consequently the problem in their case was one of social acceptance. A large number of villages in Gujarat have passed through such an initial phase.

The Harijans with *sadhan*, who benefited immensely with the opening up of dairying opportunities, consisted of an ethnic group called the Venkars. In terms of traditional social hierarchy, they were regarded as untouchables. This is because they made use of the animal gut in order to pursue their traditional occupation of weaving. Such a lowly means of making their living brought down their social status below the traditional line of touchability.

The Venkars deeply resented such a classification and continually made efforts, both educational and economic, to get out of such a stigma. But nothing worked. Moreover, the rise of the textile industry had very nearly taken away their traditional means of livelihood. Even when the Venkars ceased to be weavers their classification as weaver untouchables, in the traditional hierarchy, continued.

In the meanwhile their emphasis on education has been so great that they are about the most widely, and even highly, educated group in a number of rural communities in Gujarat. In most villages Venkar males, and in some cases females, can read and write. And in most village schools, the performance of their children is also among the top few. The social treatment of the Venkars of Gujarat is thus way out of line with their individual personal attainments.

When the dairying opportunity opened up for the Harijans in the villages of Kaira, the Venkars took to it in a big way. A number of villages reported that their milk production per capita, and the fat content within it, was about the highest. In 1961–62 we had noticed a few buffaloes 'parked', as it were, in front of Venkar homes in the village of Asodar. In 1972–73 we were in that village again for the next round of our research update. The number of 'parked' milch animals this time around simply astounded us. There was literally an overcrowding in the space with far too many buffaloes tied to the front yards and sides of Venkar homes. Some of the mud homes had gone, instead there were houses made of bricks. So very impressive was the milk productivity of the Venkars that the organizers of the village coop spoke about them in the most flattering terms. Only a few years ago the same organisers were not very keen on letting them into the village coop itself.

The final question in this connection was how very great was Amul's effort in converting the landless into milk producers. To begin with such an effort called for the conversion of a part of village *gauchar* (common grazing land) into a fodder farm for growing fodder for the animals of the landless. The existing *gauchars*, in almost all villages, are sadly neglected and are of very little use. But such a scheme brought Amul face to face with the state bureaucracy which alone had the authority to give permission for such a transformation.

With great difficulty Amul got permission to set up community fodder farms in eight villages of the district. Out of those, unfortunately, only two served their intended purpose. The remaining six turned the fodder cooperative for the poor into a resource for only those who could afford the price of it.

For the landless then the only resource left was that of *bharo*, a headload of farm cuttings which the employers allowed to the average farm worker as a part of the wages. While *bharo* had become an accepted part of the wages, the landless could not always bank on it. Apart from the fact that not all the employers liked the idea of such a payment in kind, there was always a lot of hassle every evening before the headload actually left the farm. Then there was the problem of its availability during certain seasons. The farms which had good supply of water and/or were close to canals could provide it almost all the year round.

Amul, for its part, remained far too occupied with larger organizational issues to worry about who it had yet to enrol in order to reach out to its poor. Moreover, it needed an extraordinary determination to target the unreached poor as the next challenge to be faced, especially at a time when its own productivity figures, which were bound to generate complacency, were so very impressive. Nothing in its original intent was there to compel it to do something for those voiceless poor who were not heard for centuries.

Nor could Amul compel the village milk coops to come up with alternative ideas for reaching out to their own poor. In fact most of those organisers showed a surprising degree of indifference to their own poor. In rural India one is so very used to seeing poverty around that one often forgets that something needs to be done about it. Since the dawn of Indian civilization there have always been the socially condemned whose condition is often rationalized by others, and also by themselves, in terms of a *karmic* rationale. If they are poor, it is because of what they did in previous births, and therefore you can do nothing for them.

In the winter of 1988, however, Amul was agonizing over its flagging élan, and also over the fact that it was not doing enough for all those it had not reached out to. It began to realize that it could no longer boast of milk productivity, and that in the last analysis it will be judged for what it was able to do, and not do, for the poor and the very poor of rural India. Since it is the most efficient economic organization working in rural India today it was going to be judged by a far more severe standard than other organizations. And no matter what, *it* was expected to have all the answers to the problems of rural India. While its organizers in their individual capacity had already started working in that direction, as an institution it had yet to launch a massive effort to convert the milk have-nots into the milk haves.

The organizers of Amul were also aware of the fact that it will receive very little credit for the prolonged period of trial and error which it had to go through before it could perfect a cooperative framework which could then be adopted in the rest of the country. Such a framework, in fact, helped those dairies which came after it to skip, literally, several decades of trial and error. Such a shortened time-span also helped the other dairies to move more effectively into other fields including paying more attention to their poor. Nevertheless, Amul, as the pioneer in the field, was likely to be judged, in the final analysis, not by what it had achieved but by what it had not.

SOME RURAL COMMUNITIES

Let us now briefly examine some of the rural communities within the district where, under the impact of cooperative dairying, complex and continuing social change was generated in different compartments of their lives. We have had a look at some of those communities on a longitudinal basis stretching back nearly two decades.

Ode

In the hierarchically ordered social organization of India, any ethnic struggle for human dignity and social equality is bound to involve, sooner or later, all major public institutions of the community, including the milk coop. Such a social involvement on the part of the coop, if it takes place at a certain level of economic development, will serve a twin purpose: continued advancement and ethnic reshuffling, the latter specially through the representative mechanism of the coop. In this section we shall identify the dual purpose served by the milk coop in the rural community of Ode, and then point out how an ascendant ethnic group refused to permit similar access to other ethnic groups traditionally below it.

One of the most prosperous communities in the district is Ode. It has now grown into a small town. Its income from the sale of milk constitutes a small proportion of its total agricultural income, which comes primarily from cash crops such as tobacco and cotton. While villages surrounding Ode had their own milk coop, the rich farmers within the community had successfully resisted the idea of having one in Ode. Whenever small landowners or seasonally employed labourers approached the leaders with a request for a milk coop, they were invariably told that such an organization would not be in the best interest of the poor. The rich farmers bought milk from the milk producers, made ghee for themselves, and gave away the *chhas* (butter milk) free of charge to the poor. The rich therfore claimed that to the poor of the village, the *chhas* was a great source of nourishment.

The *chhas* argument was essentially phoney. At the root of it there was an unwillingness on the part of the rich farmers to have a milk supply of their own. What they wanted instead was a regular and inexpensive supply of milk from those who maintained milch animals. Consequently, the milk producers of Ode had to wait for a number of years until the ethnic divisions among the rich farmers themselves led to the establishment of the coop.

The inauguration of the milk coop in Ode came at the climax of a prolonged ethnic struggle for power and status between the two segments of the Patels. The Patels of Ode were divided into the Patidars, the local residents, and the Kanbis (the migrant labourers who came to work on the farms of the Patidars a long time ago). For a number of years the Patidars considered the Kanbis their social inferiors, a status which the Kanbis deeply resented. In 1951, when the electoral roll for the first general election in India was under preparation, the Kanbis petitioned for the dropping of the word 'Kanbi' in front of their names. Like the Patidars, they too wanted to be known as Patels.

Then there was a change in the landowning status of the Kanbis which helped them to push their claims to a higher status and control of public institutions. By the early 1960s, the bulk of the Kanbis, who worked as tenants on the farms of Patidars, came to acquire very fertile tracts of Patidar land under the land Tenancy Act. Under such a shift nearly half of the Patidar land came in their possession. The Patidars, as could be expected, reacted angrily. They now wanted to check all the avenues of Kanbi advancement. They also wanted to keep them out of all public institutions. The Kanbis for a long time could not make much headway in the local panchayat. It was against such a background that the Kanbis decided to listen to the clamour of the milk producers, particularly from the lower social strata, for a milk coop.

Earlier the Patidars had opposed the idea of Ode having a milk coop. Such an opposition gave the Kanbis a free hand with its establishment. Still they wanted to be secretive about it. What they did therefore was to enlist most of the Kanbis as shareholders, with a few from the socially lower strata of society, and approached Amul for all the formal paper work. Amul at that stage did not want to get involved in the internal power struggle of Ode so it acted strictly according to its byelaws and gave recognition to the Ode milk coop. This was the second time the Kanbis of Ode had pulled a fast one on its Patidars. The latter could only fume and fret but could not stop the Kanbis from presiding over their brand new milk coop. Now it was the turn of the Kanbis to keep the Patidars out of a major public institution such as the milk coop. In order to see that the Patidars did not find any excuse to get in, they simply closed the doors on the enrolment of new members.

The tragedy of this was that such a move also excluded the socially and economically lower groups of Ode's society. The Kanbis apparently had a very short memory. They forgot what it was like to be excluded from public institutions and circles of respectability. They also forgot their days of toil and struggle when they worked on the farms of Patidars as landless labourers. Now that they had made good for themselves they did not have to worry about those in the social queue behind them.

Twelve years later, in 1986, the ferocity of the ethnic warfare between the Kanbis and the Patidars had not abated. Nevertheless, the Kanbis were far more secure economically and even socially than before. They had totally dropped the term Kanbi and had preferred to be addressed as Patels or even Patidars. However, such a one-sided assumption of respectability and self-promotion did not sit well with the Patidars of the village who believed that once a Kanbi always a Kanbi, and that people do not become respectable by adopting respectable surnames. After all much greater transgression in surname adoption had occurred when Harijans and other lower social groups had taken classic Rajput surnames. The only thing the Patidars could do now, in order to reinforce the social distance, was to bring back the prefix before their names and insist on being called 'Leva' Patel rather than plain Patel. In the context of the village, so as not to be mixed up with the new, and from their point of view pseudo Patels, they preferred to address themselves as Leva Patels or Leva Patidars.

The Leva Patidars, however, had a major disadvantage. A large number of them had moved to urban centres where they had either undertaken commercial or industrial ventures or had joined some profession or firms. Only a few of them were left behind in the village to look after their landed property, whatever was left of it. The migrants were under constant fear of losing more land. Consequently, they visited Ode as many times as they could, indicating that that was still their principal residence.

Such a semi-migratory condition had prevented the Leva Patidars from giving a good fight to the new Patels. While the former were literally excluded from the milk coop, they gave the latter a taste of their own medicine by excluding them from the panchayat office-bearer positions.

In this game of power and status, the net losers were those who did not have anything to do with the internal cleavage of the Patels. The Kshatriyas, Harijans and other disadvantaged groups waited endlessly for their entry into the village milk coop, and their turn did not come until 1986 when, at long last, Amul moved into the fray. It quoted the laws of the state which stated that an application for membership to a public body cannot be ignored for more than two months after being received. That meant that in the days to come the character of public institutions of Ode was likely to undergo radical changes.

The Leva Patidars and the new Patels, together, were only one-fourth of the village population. Out of nearly 3500 households in Ode, theirs, together, were only 800. But the remaining households were so very fragmented, and a number of them worked as employees on the farms of the Patidars; they therefore had no courage openly to defy their employers.

Amul from a distance watched, perhaps a little too long, the helplessness of the poor of Ode who were bottled up in a special category of 'nominal' members, whose milk was collected, and who were given bonuses, but were deprived of voting rights. By 1987 it was able to persuade the Ode milk coop to open up its membership to others. It now remains to be seen what changes take place in the public institutions of Ode including its milk coop in the years to come.

Asodar

In a perceptive paper, Raymond Firth, the anthropologist, argued that in smaller units of operation farmers are often able to make rational economic decisions. In his words, '. . . in the microeconomic sphere peasants are well aware of the possibilities of rational economic actions and make strong endeavours to better their economic positions'.[4] This observation was borne out by our case-study of the village of Asodar, especially with reference to the working of its milk coop. Situated nearly thirty kilometers from Anand, the village has a population of more than 6500 people. In recent years, the availability of water by means of a network of canals, all around, has transformed the agricultural scene of the village.

Asodar is an overwhelmingly Kshatriya village, and when universal adult suffrage was introduced in its panchayat, the Kshatriyas got control of it. But their entry and control of the panchayat through competitive politics had left behind its own consequences on the inter-ethnic relationships within the community.

But that, however, was not the case so far as the milk cooperative in the village was concerned. From the early years of its establishment, the villagers made a decision not to drag their conflicts based on ethnic divisions into the coop. Such a resolve remained unabrogated.

The people of Asodar maintained that the milk coop, as an organization, was their means of livelihood and economic development and therefore ought to be managed by those who were likely to run it with utmost efficiency. By contrast, the same people did not feel the need to conform to such a self-imposed discipline when the panchayat was in question. The panchayat thus became an arena for the expression of one's power and status drives, whereas the milk coop remained an organization for getting the best returns, in tangible economic terms, for one's milk output.

The village received its milk coop in the early years of Amul, and that was in 1956. Earlier it had tried its hand at various kinds of coops, but each time the intense ethnic conflicts between the two agriculturist castes in the area, namely, the Patidars and Kshatriyas (over land, social status and political power), had wrecked the possibility of a cooperative venture. Such conflicts were also reflected in all other public bodies, including the panchayat.

Of the two contending groups, the Kshatriyas, being economically more backward, had a greater need for the milk coop, and at the time it came into existence, the young Kshatriya leadership, which happened to be the one in power in the panchayat, was able to work out an operative relationship with an equally young Patidar leadership across the ethnic divide. Together they prepared the groundwork for the milk cooperative in the village.

When the milk coop finally came into existence, the large number of Kshatriya shareholders could have elected its officers from among their own ranks, but they did not. Instead they elected Banias or Brahmins or Patidars, all of whom are supposed to have, at least from the point of view of the Kshatriyas, a better understanding of how to operate an economic institution to one's maximum advantage. During each coop election, the average Kshatriya showed a preference for someone who would enhance his economic interests, rather than a mere kinsman.

Functionally speaking the two public bodies, the panchayat and the milk coop, catered to the two different needs of the village. Unlike the bureaucratically well-oiled machine of the milk coop, where very little was left to human chance, the panchayat had remained a scene of spontaneity and confusion. As opposed to the cold statistics and the ledger-bound world of the milk coop, the members of the panchayat often engaged in guesswork while trying to solve their problems. Despite this the panchayat complemented the rigidly structured situation of the milk coop. The members of the panchayat seemed aware of the wide range of freedoms which the institution had conferred upon them, together with a relatively higher formal status and substantive village-wide powers vis-à-vis the milk coop. While the coop imposed rigid discipline in the name of the economic interests of its shareholders, the panchayat became an arena for a search for human dignity and equality which was often mistaken for squabbling.

What was extraordinary in all this, however, was the distinction which the same group of villagers had learned to make whenever they switched from one institution to another. Temporally speaking, the milk coop had come after the panchayat; nevertheless, it had succeeded in driving home the substantive difference between the two public institutions.

While the villagers needed the milk coop for a part of their livelihood, they also needed the panchayat as an instrument of ethnic reshuffling, especially for the middle and the lower ethnic groups in the village which were beginning to register some degree of social mobility.

The Kshatriyas, despite their search for a higher social status than what was accorded to them by the social hierarchy of the village, had learned not to use the representative mechanism of the milk coop for their social objectives. As a group they used the panchayat for their status drives but refrained from using the milk coop for a similar purpose.

Over the years the coop had succeeded in inculcating the need to make a rational distinction between the two different public institutions as such. After the establishment of the coop in the village, the earlier tendency of indiscriminately running down the public institution had tapered off. There was now praise for the work which the milk coop had done without attempts at harsh comparative judgements as to the performance of other public bodies.

Over the years, the average shareholder in the village had also perceived the need to run the milk coop by means of a different set of rules than those he had adopted in other institutions. Such a separation within a common democratic process of the community was indeed a great step forward. As a matter of fact, it reflected the growing maturity of judgement of the villagers based on a rational estimate of priorities for the working of different public institutions. In all this the milk coop itself had played no small part in making a rational discrimination of priorities possible.

In the mid 1980s, the village of Asodar, agriculturally, had come a long way indeed. The network of canals and waterducts had made plenty of water available to the farmers. By this time the village had enjoyed nearly a decade of agricultural prosperity. That in turn changed the cropping pattern, the duration of the employment of the landless and, because of the availability of grass and farm cuttings to the landless, the nature of dairying itself in the village.

Asodar's traditional crops of bajara, tobacco, kodara, wheat, etc., came to be supplemented by means of vegetables, sugar cane, bananas and potatoes. Bananas in particular were now grown all the year round and were a source of substantial additional income for the farmers. It was estimated that the local banks had received a deposit of Rs6m in 1985 alone. This for a village of 6500 people (in 1981) was indeed a remarkable achievement.

The explosive agricultural growth of the village in recent years had also provided its landless with farm work almost all the year round. Such work also entitled the landless to a *bharo* of farm cuttings almost on an assured basis as there was plenty of it. That in turn opened up the possibility of the landless being able to maintain a milch animal.

Hardly a decade ago, the landless could not get work for more than four to five months in a year. In the mid 1980s the farmers were complaining of the shortage of agricultural labourers. Sometimes they had to pay wages in advance so as to book, on time, increasingly scarce farm help.

As a rule the farm worker received Rs10 per day, plus one midday meal, two teas, bidis, and one *bharo* of farm cuttings. Most landless workers went out to work with their spouses and small children, and with two workers working a full day, and in some cases a grown-up child working a half day, an average family took home upward of Rs500 a month.

In 1984–85, nearly fifty landless labourers applied for loans for animals to the local bank. The village coop undertook to collect the instalments. And it thus added more milk producers to its roster, this time around it included those who had had no hope of becoming milk producers.

With this new kind of member coming in, Asodar milk coops registered a quantum jump in membership, from 792 in 1983–84 to 1041 in 1984–85, thereby adding 249 members in one year alone. From the point of membership that indeed was the best year for the village milk coop.

In terms of milk collection, as could be expected, Asodar milk coop had also come a long way. In 1965–67, its annual collection was 180,000 litres. That jumped to a hefty 630,000 litres in 1985.

While there was all-round improvement in the economic condition of the various ethnic groups in the village, that of the Venkars had registered a relatively greater improvement. And a part of the reason for this was their access to dairying.

Over the years, the Venkar work ethic had not abated in its intensity. Even when most of them owned small pieces of land, in their spare time they preferred to work on the farms of others and thereby added to their income. The same was true of their involvement in dairying. They continued to multiply the number of milch animals and went on increasing their subsidiary income from the sale of milk. And as stated earlier, their hope was that by improving their economic condition, and also by emphasizing education, they would be able to earn greater respect from their fellow beings, and some day, a higher social status. The Venkars' means of social mobility then was hard work in agriculture and dairying along with the education of the young and old.

Since the Kshatriyas outnumbered most other social groups in the village, with all the squabbles within their ranks, they continued to control the village panchayat. Then so far as the chairmanship of the milk coop was concerned, as stated earlier, their emphasis was on the best economic managers, which in this case, in recent years, was a Patidar. They went on re-electing him over a decade despite an all-round atmosphere of ethnic hostility between them in the village, the district and the state.

A similar phenomenon, of a majority ethnic group allowing an individual from a minority group – despite wider conflicts between the two over economic interest, social status and political power – was also in evidence in Uttersanda, a village near the town of Nadiad.

Nadiad over the years had emerged into a thriving middle-sized town. Its prosperity was partly due to the Patidar agriculturists in nearby villages, who after doing well in agriculture had encouraged a member of their family to start a commercial or industrial venture in Nadiad. The family or the joint family was thus breaking out into new avenues of economic advancement without giving up its agricultural base in the village. While one of the brothers, cousins, sons or sons-in-law went into such an undertaking in the town, the others retained a base in agriculture and acted as a conduit for funnelling surplus resources from agriculture or acted as a cushion, from time to time, against the ups and downs in urban ventures.

The result was that both segments of the rural–urban family benefited. While the urban entrepreneurs took all the necessary risks, in relative terms, knowing full well that the family in the village will always bail them out, and support them till they finally succeeded, the rural component acquired the benefit of information about laws and policies, political and administrative contacts, skill in influencing and manipulating people, the education of children, and above all some measure of social and economic aggression which is difficult to acquire locally, given the complex web of traditional social relationships in rural communities.

The rural component thus added those advantages to its pre-existing economic strength, and thereby proved to be far too formidable against its local rivals. Against such a rural–urban strength the only hope for the economically weaker, and entirely village-based, ethnic groups was in their own numbers, which in turn put an enormous premium on their continued social cohesion. Whenever their factional differences got the better of their need to remain united, the rival economically powerful group, with all the advantage of urban connections, prevailed in public institutions and in the political arena in general.

That is precisely what had happened in Uttersanda. Its milk cooperative – which was the only one of its kind the villagers boasted, was inaugurated by Dr Kurien in the early days of Amul in 1951. Its population is 60 per cent Kshatriya, a numerical strength which was also reflected in their membership of the milk coop. Ever since its inception, the Kshatriyas looked after its management. But in 1975–77 they ran into difficulty with the powerful rural–urban linked ethnic group of Patidars. The Kshtriya management had continually come up with poor performance in terms of the maintenance of accounts and distributions of bonus. The Patidar leadership with its urban link threatened them with court cases. The Kshatriya leadership capitulated. And since 1977–78 the Patidars have stayed in power despite their group being in the minority. The performance of the milk coop has improved phenomenally and the Kshatriyas do not want to disturb it. They know they can come back any day, but would that help them or their fellow poor of the village? So the traditional ethnic hostility between the Patidars and Kshatriyas in the milk coop is resolved by considerations of superior economic management.

In a sense the Uttersanda phenomenon is a variation on Asodar. The latter handed over the management of the milk coop to its most efficient managers regardless of the ethnic group to which they belonged. In the case of the former, however, after an initial ethnic political conflict, a minority group stayed in power on the strength of its superior managerial performance. While the bulk of the village milk coops in the district remain under the chairmanship of the majority ethnic community, there are also those like Asodar and Uttersanda where the rational considerations of efficiency in management have prevailed over ethnic considerations.

Khadgodhara

For a long time, women in a real sense have been the principal managers of the milk economy in various societies but rarely have they been given credit for it. Moreover, when it comes to electing representatives to the various bodies connected with dairy organization and management, women are often pushed into the background.

The rural community of Khadgodhara tried to remedy such a situation. It got its opportunity to do so in the most unexpected manner. Situated nearly 60 km from Anand, Khadgodhara is in one of the backward subdistricts of Kaira. Because of its past notoriety for being a haven for criminals, even the administrators avoided going there for their routine visits. From such a position Khadgodhara, a community of nearly 1400 people, has indeed come a long way. What women did there, especially in connection with dairying, put it on the map of the dairying community in western India.

Before Khadgodhara came to have its own milk cooperative, there was another one in an adjoining village. The villagers, and particularly their womenfolk, did not like the idea of having to walk more than a mile through winding lanes in between farms, twice a day, and deliver milk to the milk coop of another village. What they wanted instead was their own milk coop. Moreover, a large proportion of the village community consisted of Muslims, and they were, given their highly restrictive views on women's movements and activities, much more opposed to the idea of their women going elsewhere even when the latter moved in groups. Consequently the villagers, under the leadership of a Brahmin widow, decided to approach the Amul officials in Anand.

In the beginning the officials at Anand were opposed to the idea of having yet another milk coop so close to the one that was already there. But looking at the enthusiasm of the villagers, and in particular of the Brahmin lady, they decided to find a way out. The only justification they could come up with was that if the proposal for a milk coop for Khadgodhara were to state that the organization would be managed entirely by women then it might be received sympathetically. To the surprise of the officials, and the delight of the Brahmin lady, the answer was an instant 'yes'.[5]

The next problem then was how to go about it. There was no preceding experience for such an organization in the district. Consequently, the rural community of Khadgodhara had to come up with their own approach to it. From the very start they decided that right from the shareholders up to members of the executive committee and chairman the milk coop should consist of women. Such an unmixed gender composition appealed to the more conservative males of the village and in particular to the Muslims. They, and in particular the latter, felt assured of the institutional insulation of their women. In actual practice, however, that was not the case, but more about that later.

The women of Khadgodhara went about their business in the most enthusiastic fashion. They knew that they were being watched and their performance unsympathetically scrutinized by the doubting males. For the men the whole thing was absurd and they expected it to fail within weeks. For the women themselves it was a moment of truth. They had to succeed no matter what. Such determination transformed the women from different ethnic backgrounds into one cohesive, and committed, group with a level of efficiency not normally seen in an organization of that kind. Some of them even neglected their household chores and family and spent an inordinately long time worrying about, and finding solutions to, the operational problems of the organization. Having boldly entered man's traditional domain of formal organization and status, it was much more important for them to succeed in what they had undertaken to do collectively, and their obsession with success shielded them from potential divisiveness until such time when the very reassurance of their success began to generate internal competition for power and status.

Between the men and women of the village no conflict arose because of the coop, at least not until 1985–86. Rather, the fact that the women had constituted their own organization gave them the assurance of a free hand within the other public body, namely, the panchayat. They were also happy that their women had something to do on their own. However, the real test of such an assurance came when the evolving public life of Khadgodhara began changing the gender composition of public bodies from an unmixed to a mixed one. While by law the composition of the milk coop had to be entirely of women, the veterans of the milk coop, who wanted to continue their activity in the public domain, started knocking at the doors of the panchayat. It was such a traffic, of the women veterans of the democratic process within the milk coop, that the men within the panchayat feared and resented the most.

The women of Khadgodhara in one decade had come a long way. Their baptism into the democratic process, through the secure confines of the all female composition of the milk coop, had politically emboldened them. Gone were the days when they could be satisfied with the jurisdiction of the milk coop reserved for them.[6] They now wanted more. Such boldness did not sit well with the male villagers. Earlier they had, albeit mistakenly, thought that they had solved the gender jurisdictional problem by agreeing to let women have a total say in the milk coop, in return for which they would tacitly agree to keep their noses out of men's business in the panchayat.

But so far as the women were concerned such a jurisdictional solution was not good enough for them. After all there were women who were milk coop retirees, with considerable experience of running a public institution like the milk coop, with a much greater budget than that of the panchayat. Moreover, such experience had fully prepared them to participate in the democratic process of the wider community which the panchayat institutionalized. The milk coop retirees, therefore, decided to contest elections against men for general seats. There were a couple of seats reserved for women, but they did not count. Their thinking now was to stand in election as a person rather than as a woman. The men, as could be expected, waffled, fumed and screamed and also lost a few seats in the election against women. And their hurt was more than electoral.

As seen from the point of view of the men of the village, the women had become a trifle unfair. First of all they had closed the door of the milk coop on men, as the charter indicated that only women could be its shareholders and office-bearers, and then they had started casting their covetous eye on what the men had, i.e. the panchayat.

As it turned out, the men were poor electoral losers. They in turn forced their women to create obstacles in the milk coop for the friends of precisely those women who had given them an electoral licking.

The reverberations of the gender-competitive politics in the village also had its toll among the women themselves. When the leadership of milk coop passed into the hands of women who were socially not high enough or educationally not impressive enough, there were a lot of unfair comments behind their backs and the pronouncements of 'What can she do? She is only good enough to be a housewife.' Worse still, 'Who would listen to her, she is not from a high enough caste.' As long as the leadership was with a Brahmin and a Brahmabhatt lady, the milk coop was supposed to be in safe hands. It was also all right when it passed on to women who were selectively groomed by these two. But when a Kshatriya and after her a Muslim lady refused to become anybody's protégée, some of the veteran retired women leaders started belittling the capacity of those two newcomers to learn and manage the institution of the milk coop.

The women of Khadgodhara thus did what the men before them had done, namely, debunk the capacity of individuals from the traditionally lower social strata to be able to manage public institutions. Luckily for the unpatronized women leaders, the performance of the milk coop did not diminish in any way.

Again, like the men before them, the women leaders did not have much confidence in the ability of the younger generation either. And such a lack of confidence had driven them to take away the opportunity of the following generation to shoulder its responsibility in managing public institutions. The younger women, and some of them from relatively lower social strata, came, nevertheless, thanks to the electoral process.

The various communities that we examined in this section thus presented a variety of insensitivity, on the part of those who got into public office, towards social segments which were socially and economically below them. The Leva Patidars did not want the Kanbis of Ode to get anywhere near a public office. Then it was the turn of the Kanbis of Ode to play the game of social exclusion against the various ethnic groups that were traditionally lower than them. The same was true also of the women of Khadgodhara. They too equated political capacity with higher ethnicity. Thus men and women of rural India engaged themselves in the game of social exclusion, with all the traditional, *karmic* and educational rationale to support their pre-judices. They behaved as Indians have always behaved since the dawn of their civilization, that is by closing down the access to advancement and status for social groups socially below them.

Such an observation also meant that you could not leave rural communities to themselves to reach out to their own poor. Invariably in them those already in power, even if they came from a formerly deprived group, as in the case of the Kanbis of Ode, developed an insensitivity, distaste and even fear of those who were socially and economically behind them.

Those organizers of Amul, who were closer to grass-roots situations and institutions, realized it and agonized over it. But those who sat only behind their desks were mesmerized by the most impressive productivity figures and told themselves that they must be doing something right or else the figures would not add up that way. Such organizers needed to be reminded what Robert McNamara said: 'It is becoming increasingly clear that the critical issue within developing countries is not simply the pace of growth, but the nature of growth.'[7] But then it would also be tantamount to asking India's premier milk cooperative society to undo what the caste system of more than three thousand years did to it, and all that in a few decades.

INTERDEPENDENCE OF TECHNOCRATS AND POLITICIANS

In organizing, operating, and extending milk cooperatives, the technocrats and politicians depended on each other. In the evolution of their interdependence the top men on both sides, i.e. technocrats (managing director and his/her senior associates), and politicians (chairman and board of directors) played a vital role. They set the pattern of mutual cooperation, implicitly understood the unstated boundaries of jurisdiction and tacitly agreed to subordinate and superordinate respective positions and decisions in specific areas where both groups were equally involved.

Since the actual operation of a dairy organization was a matter of management and engineering upkeep, the technologists assumed an important role in it. Moreover, unlike the politicians, whose electoral and party fortunes changed all the time, the technologists were immune from such uncertainties. Consequently, the latter always had the scope and opportunity to consolidate their position and strength, vis-à-vis the shifting group of politicians. Being relatively more secure in their positions than the politicians, the technocrats often cultivated effective links of communication with the bureaucracy and with politicians at the state level and with New Delhi. Such links often helped them to bypass the district level politicians in certain matters. At the same time, however, in matters of general policy they had to live within the framework of certain politically-motivated decisions imposed by the politicians despite their assured ascendancy in a wide range of matters.

The initial years of Amul were fraught with squabbles among the politicians themselves. Apart from their personal rivalry, the result of competition of political power in various public organizations within the district, there were genuine differences among them on the question of the general direction of the new organization. TK wanted Amul to become a cooperative organization of the milk producers. In his view, since the organization was for the milk producers, they should have the maximum say at all levels of its organization. Natvarlal Dave (ND), a highly-respected district-level political worker, who even went to prison during the farmers' satyagraha, thought otherwise. ND felt that Amul should become a cooperative of milk collectors. The dispute went to Morarji Desai for arbitration. Desai favoured TK's position. But the clash did not end there. The hostility between TK and ND began affecting several other organizational decisions. Finally, ND was eased out of the organization and later on from the Congress Party itself. After a few years in the political wilderness, and after experiments in political opposition to the Congress, ND, a freedom fighter, social worker and a Gujarati literary figure of considerable significance, withdrew himself from the public domain a bitterly disappointed man. Very few people talked about him and his contribution to the early days of the dairy industry in Gujarat. But then history is always about the victorious and not about those who put forward a rival point of view and failed.

The emergence of TK as a major figure in district politics, with all the vertical links with politicians in the state and in New Delhi, and with the firm belief that the milk producer should be the sole basis of a cooperative organization, was of inestimable value to Amul. Had the ND style philosophy won out, the nature of the cooperative movement in India would have been very different. It is unlikely that it would have been as effective as it was under the philosophy of a democratically operated milk producers' coop which Amul symbolized and tried to replicate in other parts of India.

TK's hands were further strengthened by the recruitment of Kurien, a brilliant engineer with a gift for building vast organisations on highly pragmatic lines. Kurien brought in his own like-minded associates, and, in particular, H. M. Dalaya. Together, and with their technocratic genius, they translated the hazy, populistic cooperative philosophy of Sardar Patel, Morarji Desai and TK into an organizational reality of great effectiveness and acclaim.

The infant organization of Amul received a great boost when the new government of Bombay, after independence, repealed its contract with the privately run Polson dairy and asked it, a farmers' cooperative, to supply milk to the city of Bombay.

Ironically enough, one of the greatest contributions of TK was to play down the role of the politicians, including himself, in the day-to-day running of Amul dairy. Right from the start he either involved the technocrats in major decisions or left decision-making in important as well as unimportant matters solely to them. In their nearly thirty years of work together, TK rarely interfered with what the technocrats wanted. He even defended them from wiley politicians and their politically motivated schemes. The technocrats in return expressed deep gratitude and proved worthy of his trust by building one of the best-known milk cooperatives in the word.

Under TK the technocrats came to have a free hand. In 1953 UNICEF, together with New Zealand, offered aid to Amul in providing free milk to children. In 1955 Amul earned visibility in the Indian market by bringing out the famous Amul butter. Later, in 1961, it produced baby food, and in 1962 made cheese out of buffalo milk which the experts from abroad thought was not possible. Subsequently, it added other products such as ghee, milk powder, high protein food, chocolate, etc., and became a household word throughout the country.

Along with its expansion, Amul continued to provide various benefits to the farmers in the form of highly-balanced cattlefeed, animal health care, facilities for artificial insemination and high milk-yielding cross-bred cows.

In almost all the villages of Kaira district, cooperative societies, managed on democratic lines, sprang up and the exposure of the farmers to the organisation and technology of modern dairying stimulated a wide range of changes in other compartments of their social and economic life. The changed outlook along with a substantial supplementary income, which small landowners in villages began to receive, were very effective contributions to rural dvelopment and to reaching out to some of the poor.

As Amul grew in stature and recognition, as an organization which had helped the milk producers, and had also enabled some of the landless to join the milk producing community in various villages, the bargaining hand of the technocrats within the organization vis-à-vis the politicians was strengthened still further. By 1962, by which time Amul had emerged as an effective organization which had done so much for the district, the politicians were inclined to agree to most of the things which the technocrats wanted.

Still the politicians could not be totally written off, not in democratic India, where there are lasting reminders of the longest freedom movement in recent history. They survived their secondary position, and at times did not fail to assert themselves effectively.

Admittedly Amul dairy, in its formative years, owed its goal, perspective and direction to the politicians. They organized and led the struggle of the milk producers against the unjust monopoly regulations foisted on them during the alien rule. While Sardar and Desai spoke vaguely of a cooperative of milk producers, TK, ND and Bhagvandas, Kishibhai, Goverdhanbhai, Prabhubhai etc., all of whom had come through the struggles of the Indian national movement, thought through the problem of actually building the organization from a basic village unit spread over nearly one thousand villages. And despite a number of squabbles amongst themselves, they went into the villages and mobilized public support for the new organization.

But that was as far as they could go. The problems of an industrial plant – with pasteurization facilities and chilling centres, engineering equipment for manufacturing milk products,milk collection and milk testing for its fat content, payment of cash twice a day, transportation, veterinary services, artificial insemination, balanced cattlefeed, and above all packaging and marketing – were all beyond them.

Once a village was inducted into the cooperative network, the responsibility of the politicians shifted to problems relating to communication of grievances and the building of working relationships with the municipality, fellow politicians, party organizations and the state government. It was in these highly specialized areas, for which the technocrats had neither the acumen nor the time nor indeed the patience, that Amul often turned to the politicians. By and large the technocrats thought of politicians as a necessary evil. Naively, and frivolously, some of them even spoke of the virtue of a firmer rule possibly under an illiberal political regime when they would not have to deal with the meddlesome and corrupt politicians. In their desire to improve matters they found that the democratic process, with its numerous failings, slowed down the undertaking of highly urgent measures. But since the process was there, they adjusted their own style of action to it.

So far as the decision-making within the apex body, namely, the board of directors, was concerned, the managing director and his top associates were the only technical people around, and still the deliberations within the board reflected a near total confidence in the work of the technocrats. The board often gave a free hand to the technocrats knowing full well that most of the decisions they made were of a technical nature and therefore best left to them. Sometimes new members of the board, who either came through the electoral process or were nominees of government, complained of the lack of participation and consultation. But those complaints were often brushed aside by skillful chairmen. In the final analysis what carried the day was the continuing success of the organization right from its inception. As long as it was there, the politicians could not justifiably interfere, they merely tentatively tried.

Within the apex body, the politicians themselves, as might be expected, were not without cleavages of their own. Such cleavages were based on a clash of personality, party affiliation or a genuine difference in perspective. At such moments the technocrats were often required to play the role of arbiter. They would then indicate in broad terms the kind of policy needed, carefully avoiding the partisan political minefield and sticking to issues which would serve the public interest the best. In other words, the technocrats not only prevailed in the internal working of the organization but also became the definers of the public good. In so doing they often entered into an arena of general well-being which was the traditional preserve of the politicians. Vis-à-vis the technocrats the politicians were often in a no-win situation. They frequently had to depend on the technocrats to bail them out of paralysing political disputes. The more they argued and differed with their fellow politicians, the more they had to surrender the ultimate decision-making and formulation of policy to the technocrats.

In matters relating to the expansion of the organization, the technocrats, with their technical presentation of feasibility studies, blueprints, charts, computer printouts, etc., made points which were far above the head of the average politician. Very few of these politicians had the necessary time to study the case in advance or the ability to extract a set of rival inferences from the same data or even question the underlying assumptions of the points made.

At the same time the operation of a vast organization such as Amul, which received and processed more than a million litres of milk per day in a flush season, often created problems of a political nature which were beyond the capacity of the technocrats to solve. There were perennial demands for higher wages from Amul's highly unionized labour, threats of strikes and constant expression of union-inspired demands. In addition to that there were demands from the municipality, the local commercial and industrial elite and from the political and partisan interests operating at the state level. For the resolution of these, and many other problems the technocrats had to depend on the politicians.

Given the nature of the dairy industry, both in terms of the perishability of milk and the village-based milk producer, the interdependence of the technocrats and politicians cannot be overemphasized. The perishability of milk, unlike sugar, edible oil, cotton, tobacco, etc., required the organization to work efficiently and in accordance with the clock. Only the technocrats, given a free hand, could provide that level of efficiency.

Nonetheless, in mobilizing support for the cooperative organization at the grassroots level, at least in the early years, the importance of the politicians could not be overlooked. In the 1950s and 1960s the contribution of the politicians in that respect was indispensable. However, once the organization got itself established, the new villages did not require persuasion by politicians. That work was then undertaken by the veterinarians and their associates. They set up committees in various villages, by means of elections, and explained how the village-level organization would work. The finer points were then picked up by the villagers themselves when the scheme became operational.

The importance of the politicians, however, did not end when the organization became operational. They continued to keep an eye on the political process, which often brought into prominence different rural leaders in the farflung district organization who could then be won over to their side by means of a promise of political support. The politicians also dealt with the municipality, the trade union, the party, and the government leaders by means of the long-cultivated political skill of give-and-take and mutual accommodation.

All in all, the more the technocrats and politicians worked as a team with an acknowledged sense of interdependence, mutually-respected jurisdiction, and above all accommodation, the smoother was the functioning of the cooperative organization.

Over the years, due to a generational change, both in technocrats and politicians, there was also a change in their values, their ability to work together, and also a dilution in their sense of mission of the earlier years. The early years of Amul reflected, in its technocrats and politicians, the sterling qualities which were present in the top leadership of the Indian national movement. In everyone connected with Amul dairy there was a tremendous sense of purpose and the excitement of building the new economic institutions of a free India. Consequently, everyone went out of his way to put in that extra bit of oneself and of one's time which, cumulatively, made an enormous difference.

The technocrats over the years became more professional and began to look, far more, to the challenges of expansion rather than to a qualitative consolidation. And politicians began to look for new areas of influence, power and material gain. No one was doing any less work and yet the results in terms of looking into substantive issues and problems were not quite the same.

The generational shift was not total. There were a few surviving individuals from the early days, and the memories of the commitment of early years came back to haunt the surviving technocrats and politicians,but by that time the torch was already passed on to a new generation on both sides of the managerial divide. But instead of sitting back and agonizing in a distant corner in their declining years, the survivors prevailed in inducing an evaluation and course correction process. The year of 1986, especially, was spent in addressing themselves to those questions. And the survivors were indeed lucky to have a younger generation of technocrats and politicians who were willing to share their concerns for the future.

Amul in that respect proved to be a unique organization. It had much more resilience in it than in most other institutions which came out of the Indian national movement. In 1986 technocrats and politicians closed their ranks to address themselves to a common goal, of reviving the old spirit and dedication of reaching out to the poor in the district beyond the impressive figures of phenomenally increased milk productivity. Productivity was important, but what was equally important, and urgent, was how to involve the poor, as partners, in such an achievement and also let them share the fruits of productivity.

For Amul now the four decades old definition of the 'poor' was not good enough. Any milk producer then, who was exploited by the middlemen, was by its earlier definition a 'poor farmer'. Its need for a new definition of the 'poor' in the 1980s forced it to look at the resourceless poor of rural Gujarat, locked in a network of social relationships which heaped on them not only economic disadvantages but social indignities as well. And to reach out to them was not going to be easy for Amul. In any case free India's enormously successful institution had now an enormous challenge before it.

SOME GENERAL OBSERVATIONS

All economic and political institutions of developing countries reflect the vision and the drive of their founding fathers. Once established, those countries take it for granted that such institutions would continue to serve their original purpose and maintain the same degree of dynamism. Over the years they have sadly realized that that is not the case. And that what sustains those institutions, in the long run, is a commensurate social and political capacity of the people within them to put adequate pressure on those institutions, and on people who operate them, to stay on course.

Amul realized this in its own agonizing reappraisal, especially after its phenomenal expansion. Its network of institutions right down the line were functioning efficiently and the milk productivity itself was rising impressively. What is more its own extension work, especially among women, and its own new health programme for the members of the dairy coop in the district, was earning national and international acclaim.

Amul's health programme, in particular, was its way of reaching out to its own poor. What it could not do in the economic field, it was trying to make good in the health field. Its recently established Tribhuvandas Foundation (1979), with a highly dedicated group of doctors, nurses and health workers, had built a network of health services in more than 336 villages. For this purpose, besides other donors, a part of the cost is borne by Amul and the other part, consisting of Rs10 per family per year by way of health insurance, is borne by the members of village cooperative society.

There are a variety of highly effective services which the Foundation has undertaken to provide. These consist of the retraining of the *dais* (traditional birth attendants), the keeping of adequate records of health of mothers and babies, immunizing, providing preventive and curative medicine, giving advice on nutrition, eradicating tuberculosis, keeping records of women in the fertility group, and above all persuading women with two children to go to the Foundation's clinic for family planning.[8]

But success, and phenomenal success, brought with it the dilution of the original purpose which was to help the poor. In its place came emphasis on productivity and on plans to replicate the organization elsewhere in India. The importance of none of these could be minimized. And yet these could not, and ought not to have become the *primary* concerns of an organization which probably represented the best in free India's social concerns.

The institutional charter clearly suggested that the organization was for the milk producers only. And if somebody was not a milk producer, it was not the responsibility of Amul, officially speaking, to make him one and then bring him within the umbrella of the organization. It was the responsibility of government, and of society in general, to give him the necessary means to become a milk producer, and after that a dairy organization like Amul could take over the responsibility.

While officially that was the policy, in actual practice, directly or indirectly, extension officers and vets did get involved in the implementation of the provisions of new public policy to help the rural poor by means of giving them loans and subsidies to become milk producers. What they could not bear to see, when such a public policy was being implemented, was the ripping off of the poor by bank officials, government servants, politicians and livestock merchants, most of them of questionable integrity, benefiting by the helplessness and gullibility of the poor. For those select number of Amul personnel, however, their involvements were involvements of conscience. Moreover, such involvements, considering what was needed in the district, were few and far between.

This added an element of ambivalence. While the organization was officially concerned with the milk producers of the district, its socially concerned officials were also involved in their own limited way in helping others to become producers.

At the organizational level, Amul was also under pressure from planners, policy makers, social workers, electioneering politicians, etc., to devise new strategies to help the poor. Since as an organization in rural India it had done more for the rural population than any other body since Indian independence, it was natural for all these to approach Amul. In return it was gratified, and also proud, for the trust placed in it. Nevertheless, it did not want to make any official commitment in that direction. It welcomed new assignments such as the building of parallel organizations in other sectors of the economy, some of which were very ingenious, but that is as far as it went, at least organizationally.[9]

But restricting itself to the milk producers only was Amul's way of doing what it was good at. Because beyond that there was the complexity of caste and economic frontiers. Rural communities in India have lived far too long with the caste system and therefore regard it as a necessary part of their social and economic existence. For them there always will be those who are socially higher and lower and also economically better off and worse off. And if somebody was excluded from the basic human dignity and economic opportunity, there were traditional explanations of *karma* for it. His or her present social status had much to do with what he or she did in past births.

So very deeply institutionalized is the *karmic* rationale in rural India, in the minds and manners of both the well-provided and the deprived, that there is very little questioning of it on either side. Only the social reformers question them but then after some time they go away and life goes on as before.

The net result of living in such a social organization has been that community after community neither feels guilty nor responsible for its poor and the deprived. Each of them has been so much insensitized, and even brutalized, over centuries, that it sees the poor and the very poor as an indispensable part of its social landscape. For it the poor are there not because any social injustice was perpetrated against them but because someone higher than them, for reasons of his own, had put them there. In that respect, the entire range of efforts made by religious and social reform movements and the national movement of the last two hundred years together with the secular and enlightened policies of free India, given the immensity of the problem, had achieved precious little. The number of the poor in rural India since independence has doubled, and the *karmic* rationale justifying it has not lost its acceptability.

As long as one did not tell oneself that some are poor because others had correspondingly more than their fair share, one did not have to feel guilty about it. The poor were thus not a product of an unjust social order but only of a divine dispensation of justice. What, therefore, surprises any observer in rural communities, as it does in urban communities, is the baffling insensitivity of the people towards their own poor.

As we saw in the earlier sections, the three rural communities of the district did not show any extraordinary concern for their poor. Of the three Asodar, managed by an efficient manager, had a relatively higher concern for its poor. The rest showed as much insensitivity to them as any other rural community in the country.

How far, then, is there justification in a position which implies that each community should look after its own poor and help them acquire the ability to come out of their own economic limitations? Again and again we see that they do not. Again and again we also see that whatever has been earmarked for them either does not reach them or is so misconceived and ineffective that it fails to produce the intended results.

Such failures of others' efforts bring in an added, and sometimes unfair, share of responsibility on those development agencies which are working efficiently in rural India, i.e. the milk cooperatives of western India. The very logic of the situation thus forces them to go beyond the confines of their own official charter, namely, the milk producers. In a sense they have been asked to shoulder and thereby pay for their own effectiveness and success.

Indian society has yet to produce a mass movement, corresponding to its earlier national movement against the alien rule, which can generate leadership of the dedicated men and women who would then spread out into rural India, on a massive scale, and mobilize and organize the poor to demand, effectively, what has been provided for them in various plans and social policies, and also help them develop their social and political capacity by means of involvement in development and participatory processes and bring about their own self-development through self-involvement.

The students of society and politics of India are now beginning to understand the colossal damage done by the Indian caste system to the lower strata of its society. It simply devastated them, and even took away their will to fight back for human dignity and social justice. One has to spend only twenty-four hours in an Indian village to realize it. And solutions and development strategies which ignored this basic fact – that there is the cultural and political base to India's problem of poverty – have not worked and will not work. Caste riots and religious conflicts in the rural and urban communities of Gujarat in the 1980s, in the land of Mahatma Gandhi, forced the students of society and politics to reconsider the continued strength of social divisions based on them. Deeply enmeshed in those divisions are also the economic factors which could not be understood in their isolation.

But until the planners and strategists come out with what will work – given the network of traditional relationships, social cleavages, values and rationales – and until a massive movement for internal social change is generated, the interim responsibility falls on institutions like Amul. And there are not many of those around which are operating in an arena where the fundamental problems of poverty actually are. In the period of transition they will then have to share a much larger burden of social responsibility. Unfair as it may seem there is not much at the moment that is going for the poor and the neglected of India.

2 Dudhsagar Dairy: a cooperative miracle[1]

No other milk cooperative has been able to transform the rural economy of its district as fundamentally as did the Dudhsagar Dairy of Mehsana. While milk productivity and improvement of the quality of milch animal remained the primary goals of its organization, its policy towards women, and lately towards the poor of the district, has had a significant impact. Dudhsagar considered itself to be an offshoot of Amul, and like the latter it too was a product of the Indian national movement and social dynamism that was generated by it. Its founding father, Mansinhbhai Patel, came through the mill of the Indian freedom movement and, in the post-independence period, he turned his attention to the economic development of the district of Mehsana through the dairy industry. The district of Mehsana a few years ago was considered to be one of the backwaters of the state. And now in its dairy development, cattle improvement, and in the quality of its various programmes in general, it is likely to be a leader in the country.

The district of Mehsana was not blessed with very many natural resources. It has neither good soil nor rivers with potential for irrigation. The rainfall there is often erratic and insufficient. Consequently, before the arrival of the dairy industry, the district was considered to have limited agricultural prospects.

The only major dairying resource it has had was that of the famous *mehsani* buffalo. And Dudhsagar, with the help of the women of the district, and the vets, developed the animal to its perfection. It then moved in the direction of cross-bred cows, conducted a lot of its own research and increasingly made the more high milk yielding animals available to its inhabitants. By 1989, in less than three decades after its establishment, its productivity reached the figure of Rs1500m.[2] It thus injected into the rural economy of the district an inordinately large sum of money from the sale of milk and milk products. Such a resource then helped the farmers of various rural communities, as we shall see in this chapter, to improve their agricultural yield by using more water, better seeds, fertilizers and pesticides. It also enabled them to experiment with new crops. Moreover, it helped them to switch to high milk yielding animals which initially required much higher investment. Finally, it indirectly helped various extended families to start commercial and industrial ventures in nearby towns without giving up agriculture and dairying. Together these set in motion certain processes of social change, the impact of which is being continually felt in different compartments of rural life.

In this chapter we shall examine the growth of the milk cooperative movement in Mehsana and the consequent changes in certain rural communities in the district. The chapter is divided into the following parts: the growth of Dudhsagar dairy; range of dairy activities; involvement of women; some rural communities; and some concluding observations. We shall now examine each of these in some detail.

THE GROWTH OF DUDHSAGAR DAIRY

A large part of the district of Mehsana was governed by the enlightened princely state of Baroda. The Gaekwads of Baroda were well known for their emphasis on education, particularly of women, enlightened public policy and a relatively humane and sympathetic response to the cause of the freedom movement in colonial days. In the princely states of India the struggle for independence was waged through an organization called the Praja Mandal. The Mandal was, for all practical purposes, a counterpart of the Indian National Congress in the princely states.

The unit of Praja Mandal in Mehsana, being close to Sabarmati Ashram (40 km) – from where Mahatma Gandhi influenced, shaped, and directed the struggle for independence and its accompanying constructive programmes – could not escape its twin emphases on the mobilization of people and rural upliftment. Consequently, the youthful political leadership of the district, especially in the 1930s, had its own baptism in the importance of these two goals, and its interest in them continued throughout its public life. Such a leadership, in turn, handed over its own legacy to the generation that succeeded it. Most of the organizers of Dudhsagar dairy, in the 1970s and 1980s, belonged to a cross-section of these two generations.

Mansinhbhai Patel, the founder of the Dudhsagar dairy, belonged to the older generation. He was the son of a school teacher from a relatively less known and less important village in the district's social hierarchy. In both his school and college days he got deeply involved in student activities relating to the mobilization of people and raising their political awareness. He received his B.A. degree at Baroda College in 1942, and a law degree from Bombay University in 1945. At the young age of 26, he was elected as an MLA to represent his district in the then Bombay Legislative Assembly. From then on, until his premature death in 1970, he fully participated in – and almost always initiated – activities related to the rural development of his district.

The district of Mehsana does not have many large rivers. Consequently, for its agricultural development it had to depend, by and large, on bore wells. On his part, Mansinhbhai put enormous pressure on the government of Gujarat, and various other funding agencies, to enable the districts to have as many bore wells as possible. Subsequently, by 1989, due to the efforts of Mansinhbhai, and also because of the financial resources generated by Dudhsagar, the district of Mehsana came to have more than 10,000 bore wells. In that respect it has become one of the largest bore well operating districts in India.

In 1957 Mansinhbhai had his first, and probably only, political setback. He was opposed to the Mahagujarat movement for the bifurcation of the former composite state of Bombay. Consequently, in the assembly election of the same year he could not hold on to his elective position.

His political defeat proved to be a blessing in disguise for the district. He could now concentrate exclusively on its many-sided development. It was at that stage that he started playing with the idea of a milk cooperative organization for the district.

Already there was, before him, an example of a highly successful milk cooperative, namely Amul, in the neighbouring district of Kaira. Amul dairy had virtually transformed the agricultural economy of its own district. The question before Mansinhbhai, therefore, was whether or not he could do something on similar lines for his own district, i.e. Mehsana.

Fortunately for him the two principal makers of Amul, namely Dr V. Kurien and Tribhuvandas Patel, were also very keen on helping him. So far as the milk producers of the district were concerned, they too were most enthusiastic. In the absence of a milk cooperative dairy in the district these producers had to depend on the middlemen, and milk traders, and the volatility of manipulated market prices. Consequently, by the end of 1960, the Dudhsagar dairy was able to register itself as the milk cooperative for the district.

Like all other milk cooperatives, Dudhsagar too had a small beginning. Despite all the demonstrated enthusiasm of milk producers, before it actually came into existence, in the beginning it had the genuine commitment and support of only 11 villages. Others had adopted a wait and see approach. Dudhsagar, however, did not have to wait for long. As the effort for mobilizing support for the newly established dairy organization picked up, increasingly a larger number of villages expressed their willingness to join it. Others had to wait till their access roads, truck routes and chilling centres were ready.

Dudhsagar's big break came when the Chinese invaded the Indian borders in 1962. After that the Indian army needed a reliable supply of milk powder in large quantities. One of the dairy organizations selected for that purpose was Dudhsagar. As a result the dairy received a large grant from New Delhi to set up its own milk powder plant in 1963. The army contract thus relieved Dudhsagar from its dependence on the regional market.

In less than two decades, from 11 villages in 1961, Dudhsagar was able to bring within its cooperative framework 875 villages by 1980. By that time it had registered more than 200,000 farmers as milk producers and started collecting 500,000 litres of milk per day, in return for which it provided the district with a sizeable income. The other income of the district, which its veterinary section had significantly enhanced, was from the sale of milch animals. The *mehsani* buffalo, together with the cross-bred cow, became yet another source of the district's income.

Like Dr Kurien, of Amul dairy, one of the reasons for Mansinh-bhai's success was his unique ability to collect round himself a group of highly dedicated engineers, dairy technologists, veterinarians, procurement officers, district level politicians and, above all, farmers. These, together, effectively mobilized and rebuilt a milk producing community within a cooperative structure. Further, such a structure went beyond the routine function of collecting, processing and marketing milk. On the contrary, it attended to questions relating to cattle feed, cattle health and improvement in cattle breeding together with a wide range of social issues which cannot be separated from rural development in general.

While all these major achievements were well under way, Dudhsagar suffered its greatest loss ever. In 1970, Mansinhbhai, who was preparing to attend a conference in Sydney, Australia, died in a car accident. Nearly two decades have passed since his death, but the farmers of the district remember him with tears in their eyes. Fortunately for Dudhsagar the succeeding generation of its organizers, namely, Motibhai Chaudhuri and B.C. Bhatt also proved to be equally dedicated and effective.

Mansinhbhai belonged to an agriculturist caste called the Chaudhuries. The Chaudhuries are sometimes regarded as a separate segment of the Patidar caste and, on other occasions, as a distinct group. In a number of villages within the district there is an economic rivalry between the Patidars (Kadava) and the Chaudhuries with its inevitable overtones of claims to higher social status.

As a rule the Chaudhuries, in search of a higher economic and social status, are considered to be a hardworking people. In sheer application to work, the Chaudhuries, both men and women, excel the Patidars.

The hardworking Chaudhury community saw in Mansinhbhai a leader who could help them rise in both the economic and social scale. So far as the Patidars were concerned, after an initial round of suspicion of his phenomenal rise to power and importance, they too joined him in his effort in the economic development of the district. Through such a development, they argued, they too would stand to gain.

While the Chaudhuries, who possessed a bigger milch herd than the Patidars, gained enormously through the district-wide organization of milk cooperatives, the latter, with more land holdings, also gained in further improving their agriculture by making use of the enhanced supplementary income provided by increased sale of milk. The Patidars could now buy better seeds, more fertilizers and pesticides, and could employ more labourers to work on their farms during peak agricultural seasons. What is more, they could now spend more money on bore well facilities either by joining the existing groups of farmers who owned such wells cooperatively, or by constituting new groups for the purpose.

Their increased agricultural income also helped the Patidars to start commercial ventures in various towns of the district such as Mehsana, Patan, Sidhpur, Bijapur, Harij, etc. More and more Patidars opened shops in those towns doing business in cloth, medical supplies, automobile parts, electrical goods, grains, stainless steel utensils, etc. It was reported that by 1984, more than 90 per cent of such shopkeepers had an agricultural background, and a large number of them came from the Patidar community. And now it is only a matter of time for some of them to start small- and medium-scale industrial ventures in those urban centres.

In a sense, the Chaudhuries stood in an emulative relationship with the Patidars. Consequently, by the mid 1970s, they too had started some commercial ventures, in a limited number, in various towns of the district. From their point of view they had not yet fully exhausted their animal husbandry resources. They were very well known as the keepers of animals and often got a lot more out of them than any other group in the district. Consequently, by and large, they confined their ambition for economic expansion within what they were good at.

So far as the other social groups of the district were concerned, they are the upper caste Rajputs, Kshatriyas and Venkars. They stood in some kind of a queue of groups seeking economic development through dairying. They moved into it at the start of their economic development and their emphasis on it was likely to become less if and when they discovered more rewarding and quicker ways of development.

Then there were the traditional keepers of the animals, namely the Rabaris. The scientifically trained vets posed a great threat to them and to their livelihood. But as we shall see later on, the resistance of the Rabaris to the modern ways of keeping animals was slowly beginning to crumble.

Finally, the two social groups, namely, the Momens (Muslims) and Momins (Ismailis) who were engaged in the business of selling milch animals. Both these groups had a commercial approach to the dairy industry. They were engaged in the business of exporting *mehsani* buffalos to various parts of India and in particular to the city of Bombay. Later on we shall have more to say about their flourishing trade. Since the coming of the milk cooperative meant facilities for the health care of the animal, as well as the improvement in cattle breeding, they too were most enthusiastic about the development of the dairy industry in the district.

RANGE OF DAIRY ACTIVITIES

The Dudhsagar dairy is now ranked as one of the largest milk cooperatives in India, second only to Amul. In the flush season of winter 1982 its milk collection had reached 600,000 litres per day.

And in early January 1985 it had reached close to 800,000 litres per day.

Its leadership, right down the line, is continually involved in mobilizing the milk producers of the district towards an ever-increasing milk procurement target. For that purpose it works closely with the cooperatives. Every now and then these two groups meet at the dairy headquarters in Mehsana or in the villages. Such a consultative and problem-solving process benefits both sides. It gives them a sense of togetherness and exploration of solutions to their problems in a cooperative and concerted manner. Unlike a bureaucratic organization, where one side enjoys power and authority and the other side is made to feel that there are no rights but only favours, the fact of interdependence of both sides is brought home within the cooperative structure at every stage. Within such a situation of interdependence sometimes there are, relatively speaking, a few advantages enjoyed by one side over the other. But they are always shortlived as different situations and issues shift, back and forth, such relative advantages. Consequently, both sides are on the look out, all the time, for compromises.

Such a fundamental lesson in operating cooperative organisations reinforces the democratic process both at the district and village level. While the democratic process does stimulate competitive politics at both levels, it also imposes, particularly in this situation, constraints of practicality, of having to produce results that would serve the interests of the shareholders. To the shareholders better returns for the milk, and an assured availability of all the inputs needed, determine whether the democratically arrived at decisions and elected officials were worth the effort or not. They therefore keep applying the pragmatic test to the democratic process all the time. No matter who is in charge of running the cooperative organization at the village or the district level, the shareholders must be in charge of scrutinizing the quality of their decisions and the results which they produce. Through such a demand-response process, the shareholders have learned to protect their own interests.

Such a businesslike attitude towards the functioning of various units inside the cooperative organisation not only imposes a sobering influence on their democratic process but also makes it produce results. And since results are produced, in concrete terms, year after year, the legitimacy of the democratic process itself acquires firmer roots in the minds of the people.

Village leaders, after serving in milk cooperatives, try their hand at the sub-district and district level public bodies which too are run on democratic lines. The village cooperative, in that sense, therefore, becomes a training ground for participating in the wider democratic process of the country.

The conventional approach to getting more milk out of the milch animal consisted of feeding it with cotton seeds, cotton seed cakes, grains, etc., along with green grass and hay. Such a composite feed proved to be more expensive with uncertain results. Consequently, Dudhsagar decided to provide a balanced feed to its milk producers with an eye on its milk productive capacity. For that purpose it developed its own brand and marketed it under the name of *sagardan*. Since it proved to be very popular, Dudhsagar was forced to commission more industrial units to meet the demand.

In order to produce a balanced cattle feed, at a reasonable cost, all the milk cooperatives of Gujarat, under the leadership of the National Dairy Development Board at Anand, have pooled together their scientific resources and the results of various experiments. In the winter of 1984 they had succeeded in developing what they called a chocolate brick, consisting of hay, molasses, and other nutrients, especially to be used in dry and drought prone areas. This had produced remarkable results in experimental situations. The fact remains that these dairy cooperatives, including Dudhsagar, have taken it upon themselves to develop a balanced cattle feed with optimum results and at a minimum cost.

For the health care of the animal, Dudhsagar has established seven sub-stations, with their own veterinary staff and medical supplies, within the district. Together they are linked by means of a central radio telephone system. Consequently, at short notice, veterinary assistance can be sent to the remotest village in the district. Such a network of communication, jeeps, vets, medical supplies, etc., has profoundly influenced the thinking and attitude of the farmers in the district. No livestock ailment is now considered to be beyond human effort to cure. Consequently, before the animal finally quits, it has become, so far as the average farmer is concerned, an economic necessity and a moral obligation to try and find out what these men with modern medicine can really do.

Mehsana district, as stated earlier, has a tremendous wealth of milch animals. Its buffalo, i.e. *mehsani*, is a cross between the *surati* and the *punjabi* buffalo, and an improvement upon both of them in terms of its milk yield. So great has been the demand for the *mehsani* from the rest of the country that the district has a problem coping with it. Moreover, there is a continuing threat of losing, all the time, some of its best animals. Such a concern is repeatedly expressed by the vets as well as the dairy community in general.

Dudhsagar did not adopt a complacent attitude towards the *mehsani* simply because it was adjudged to be one of the best in the country. Since the implementation of its artificial insemination programme in the 1960s, it has been engaged in further improving the quality of *mehsani* by making available to all its artificial insemination centres the semen of pedigree buffalo. Moreover, towards that purpose, it has also established a highly advanced veterinary laboratory and a farm, with bright young scientists from all over India under the leadership of a brilliant veterinarian called Dr A. S. Dave. This unit is located in a village close to Dudhsagar and is called the Jagudan Farm. The work done on this farm has earned the recognition of dairy scientists both at home and abroad.

At the farm, Dave and his colleages have kept a painstaking record of bulls and buffalo bulls and the milk giving capacity of the mothers and sisters of those animals. Besides that they have also kept a record of the effects of changes in environment, cattle feed, and the management of pregnancy-productivity cycle on the milk yield of the animal. Their principal aim was to identify what triggers, effectively, the latent biological capability of the animal. But they are also aware of the fact that because of the involvement of a number of variables, the answer to the question of biological capability is not always the same, and that what they need, therefore, is an open-minded, pragmatic and experimental approach to be able to identify the set of causal variables within a constellation of them.

In conducting these exercises and experiments, Dave and his men have not confined themselves to their farm only. They have also involved the villagers, particularly the women, with that kind of interest. Consequently, throughout the district there has been an awareness, and cooperation in making observations, keeping records, and collecting data. The villagers also know that they will be the principal beneficiaries of such findings.

One of the interesting observations to make in this connection is the attitude of the Rabaris, the caste which is considered to be the traditional keepers of the animals. Even to this day they possess a significant proportion of the animals in the district. The experiments done at the Jagudan Farm, and also in several villages, in both cattle feed and genetic manipulation, were not lost on them. Being a nomadic and therefore a marginal community, always living with the animals and grazing them in distant fields, the Rabaris had developed a psychology of aloofness and non-involvement. What has, nevertheless, electrified and threatened them is the invasion by the modern veterinarians – who are armed with their science, scientific instruments and proven results – of their traditional domain. For a long time the Rabaris did not take the vets seriously and made fun of them. However, when they began to see the results in the cowsheds and on the weight scales in the milk collection centres, their resistance to the modern ways of looking after the animal began to crumble. Now, despite their injured pride, the belittling of techniques of animal rearing which they and their forefathers practised for centuries, and, above all, a broad philosophical rejection of interfering with the course of nature, the Rabaris have begun to take the vets seriously.

While the attempts at the improvement in the milk yielding capacity of the *mehsani* have been in progress, the district has been overtaken by a growing shift towards the cross-bred cows. In different parts of India, including the Punjab, attempts were made to cross-breed foreign animals with the indigenous so as to ensure not only the milk yield but also the survivability of the animal in tropical conditions. Consequently, different combinations of cross-breeding have come with different results.

There again, Dave and his associates had enormous success. On their farm they were able to develop cross-bred cows, by means of repeated cross-breeding under observed and controlled conditions, which gave nearly 40 litres of milk per day. In one case they even reached 47 litres. As opposed to that, the best of *mehsani* rarely exceeded 15 litres of milk per day.

The news of Dave's success created tremendous interest in the district. Orders started pouring in from farmers with requests to help them switch from buffalo to cross-bred cows. The advent of the new animal is bound not only to change the rural economy of the district but also to lead to a consequent social change in many compartments of rural life.

While the cross-bred cow, which was the product of either the indigenous and Holstein-Friesian or the indigenous and the variety developed by the Australian dairymen, was on its way in, the famed *mehsani* buffalo, which has been in the region for centuries, was not on its way out. As stated earlier, Dave and his associates were hopeful of improving its milk yield still further.

Since the cross-bred cow could start calving at the age of 25 to 26 months, the question which the vets asked was whether they could achieve a similar performance with the *mehsani* at the age of 28 months or less. This they felt they could achieve if the animal, by means of special feeding, could be made to acquire a body weight of 450 kg.

In the traditional approach the *mehsani* took nearly 48 months to reach the period of its first lactation. In the new approach it was possible to bring it down to much less. Such a manipulation would then enhance the monetary advantage to its owner and give to the *mehsani*, in the face of a new competitor, another lease of life in the district.

Through a series of such activities, the vets of Dudhsagar have made the milk-producing community of the district aware of the power of human intervention and manipulation in what was re-garded, until a few years ago, as a process on which one had no control. Now the villagers of the district confront the vets with the code number of the artificial insemination straw which, a few years later, led to a high yielding animal. Across villages they compare notes on the relative efficiency of what was administered and then make a concerted demand on the vets to help them improve the milk yielding capacity of the progeny of their animals. To conclude this section, what is happening in the district under the guidance of the vets of Dudhsagar is a fundamental change in the field of animal rearing practices with their far-reaching effect on the social and economic life of the people.

INVOLVEMENT OF WOMEN

Dudhsagar is perhaps the only cooperative which has made an official policy, and not merely a strategy, to involve more and more women in its village level operations. Women have been the actual, but not formally recognized, managers of the milk economy. They look after the milch animals, feed them, scrub them, take them to village ponds to have a dip in the water, graze them in the fields or in the village common, milk them, take the milk to the milk collection centre, and remain, almost always, present when the vets came to inspect the animals. However, when it comes to their participation in organizations dealing with milk cooperatives, either at the village or the district level, they are always pushed aside and men take over. So very deeply-rooted has been this practice that women do not even complain, barring a few rare instances, against their exclusion from public bodies.

The two social groups which are deeply involved in dairying in the district, over and above the Rabaris, are the Chaudhuries and the Patidars. And in this respect, as stated earlier, the Chaudhuries have excelled all other groups in their ability and skill in looking after the animal and in bringing it to its ultimate milk-giving capability. In achieving that distinction, their womenfolk have played a remarkable role. It is often said that they are able to establish a deep bond between themselves and their animals. They show a genuine *mamta* (mother's love) towards their animals and establish what the local residents call *athwar* (deep bondage between human beings and their animals). They even talk to their animals and understand their condition and mood by watching the movements of their eyes, ears, tail, skin, neck and jaws. In return the animals also respond to their directional words. They can make the animals calm down when agitated, move, stand still and, above all, get ready for milking. The animals recognize their voice and comply with their directional commands. There is also, it is said, a difference in the quantity of milk yield when they are milked by the women who look after them rather than by others.

The vets of the district are full of praise for the ability of Chaudhury women to look after their milch animals. Even the shrewd buyers from outside the district also want to know, apart from the milk yield of the animals, whether the animal has been brought up and looked after by Chaudhury women. That then ensures the proper upbringing and the quality of the animal.

So great has been the involvement of Chaudhury women in the upkeep of their animals that even their husbands sometimes pass snide remarks at it. In winter months, they say, the animal has the priority over the use of hot water for its morning scrub, followed by a massage with oil. Moreover, one of the perplexing sights in the villages of the district is a young calf basking in the morning sun on the cot, and an infant sleeping on a torn mattress on the floor beside it.

The Chaudhury women pick up the necessary skills in looking after the animals from their mothers. But they, however, do not stop there. They also pick up, equally effortlessly, the new techniques of animal health care, the balancing of cattle feed, and improving the quality of animal offsprings. With all their traditional love of the animal, they were the first to take an enlightened interest in the programme for artificial insemination.

For the health of the animal, in particular, the Chaudhury women have set up a standard for the rest of the milk-producing community to follow. Not only that, they, together with what they call the *doba doctor*, the vets, keep on experimenting with new feed and new techniques of improving the milk yield of the animals.

In doing all this, the Chaudhury women have added yet another role for themselves in the field of animal husbandry and that is that of a willingness to try out new techniques and new ideas and thereby stay in touch, without even formal literacy in most cases, with all the modern developments in the field. The inducement for doing so, apart from the real love of the animal, is that each successful experiment means an additional income for the family.

The top organizers of Dudhsagar have been aware of the role of Chaudhury women in the dairy development of the district. And, therefore, they wanted those women to realize that their responsibilities did not end in the cowshed but also extended to all those organizational bodies where policy decisions were made. Moreover, if the Chaudhury women could be interested in organisational matters then other women, in due course, will follow their example. Consequently, they arranged a number of seminars to interest women in organizational matters.

Then came a crisis. In the late 1970s, men in various villages started clamouring for more money for milk. The organizers of Dudhsagar maintained that the consumer in the district, and outside, would not be able to bear the proposed increase in price. But the men of a number of villages remained unconvinced. Finally, under the instigation of milk traders, men from 79 villages decided not to give milk to their village cooperatives. The organizers decided to do without the milk from those villages. Accordingly, milk cans bearing the names of those villages were withdrawn and piled up at the headquarters of Dudhsagar.

Most of the men who made the decision for non-cooperation had not consulted their womenfolk. Consequently, within 48 hours of the strike going into effect, the women of the striking villages showed up at the milk collection centres first and then gathered at the dairy lawn with their children in tow, and demanded that they be allowed to sell milk to those cooperatives in their respective villages. When the various village secretaries told them that their menfolk were on strike, their answer was that it was a unilateral decision and they, the women, were not consulted. They even threatened to beat up some of the secretaries. The secretaries ran to the headquarters and refused to return to their respective villages unless they were given permission to collect milk from these irate women. A number of trucks were commissioned, forthwith, to take back the empty cans to the villages and to resume the milk collection.

The strike did not last for more than three days. But it was an eye opener to the organizers. By now they knew who their real allies in the villages were and on whom they can depend. From then on they targeted women for all their future developments in the district.

After that Dudhsagar adopted a policy of giving a joint member-ship to husband and wife as shareholders in village milk cooperatives; such a membership had one vote. Such a provision, however, gave an uninhibited access to women to attend various meetings of those bodies. After the institution of such provisions, all the villages reported a phenomenal rise in attendance at meetings consisting mostly of women.

The other important step was the insurance scheme. The insurance on the life of the milch animal, from then on, was given in the joint name of husband and wife. They were jointly made eligible for the amount which the insurance company paid. The same principle was extended to loans for buying animals. They too were given jointly so as to ensure joint ownership from the very start.

The entry of women in various village cooperatives began to change the nature of their deliberations. The women were more inclined to keep out extraneous political considerations from the milk cooperatives. Moreover, they did not want to be overly competitive and play politics with an institution which had provided them with a steady and additional means of livelihood.

Whenever a sectional responsibility was put on them, they proved to be very serious and effective team players and stood with the whole group. That was in marked contrast with an all-men situation where a lot of sparks flew and hot air blew before everyone calmed down. The men, unlike women, were not always able to identify themselves, deeply, with their own groups.

The entry of women in institutions was in its initial stages. For the time being, Dudhsagar's extensive efforts at the consciousness-raising of its women members have been very successful. Yet within various institutions they preferred to work in groups where there were all women. Barring a few villages, women were not always comfortable in mixed situations.

The various provisions made by Dudhsagar for the participation of women had to work themselves out in actual family situations. Like all other provisions – legal, constitutional, political – their importance is realized in moments of crisis and the consequent exploration for alternative action. In this case also, family squabbles, marriage breakdowns, deaths, etc., will result, as they always do, in search of the significance of what has been provided for.

With more education and an increased sense of entitlement, the women will be able to get much more out of the existing provisions and then demand more. That will also lead to a much more realistic participation on their part. As for the moment, the Dudhsagar cooperative has made a beginning for them to have, gradually, their fair share in the dairying resources of their families.

In most societies women are an underprivileged group as compared to their menfolk. Barring in tribal societies in India, as we shall see in the next chapter, their relatively inferior status is taken for granted. What Dudhsagar was trying to do, for reasons of its own, was to give a serious jolt to the deeply entrenched gender imbalance in the traditional society and force the women and men of Mehsana to strike another gender equation.

However, in the formulation and implementation of its own policy, especially towards women, the organizers of Dudhsagar also became sensitive to the presence of women per se within the rural communities of the district. A large number of women were also in the economically backward groups, in particular in the lower castes. Given their dual disability, they too began to attract the attention of its organizers. Such women began to pose a double problem, for besides being women they were also resourcelsss. Within Dudhsagar's drive to reach out to the poor, such women were therefore the first to receive its attention. The top organizers of Dudhsagar often went in search of women in the poorer castes first, who were either widows, or deserted or destitute. They then put unrelenting pressure on the village milk coops to help them become milk producers by means of loans from the bank and also get farm cuttings at a concessional rate if such women could not work. Since the top management exercised a lot of influence on the organisation, the villagers responded to their call. Moreover, when the vets, in particular, wanted to make milch animals available to the poor on their own, they often gave preference to those who were women and also the poor. Thus the thrust of Dudhsagar's effort to reach out to the district's poor was initially guided by what they could do to women of different economic backgrounds.

SOME RURAL COMMUNITIES

Let us now take into account some rural communities in the district of Mehsana which have been influenced by different social groups and their approaches to dairying. The district of Mehsana has 1100 villages. In those villages milch animals are kept by practically all the castes in order to supplement their income.

Among the social groups which are principally involved in dairying, the Chaudhuries, as stated earlier, are at the top. They have more milch animals, proportionately speaking, than most other social groups. We shall examine their approach to dairying by taking into account what they have achieved in the villages called Pamol and Bapupura.

Next we shall examine a village called Gagaret which is dominated by Patidars. Most Patidars own sizeable pieces of land along with milch animals. They are, however, not as deeply involved in dairying as the Chaudhuries. Their interest in it is strictly economic. This is because they believe that with agriculture, and its cattle feed by-products, goes dairying. The various cuttings from the fields can always feed a few animals. But whenever they reach an optimum limit, in their milk producing capacity, they prefer to diversify their resources from dairying, as well as agriculture, to commercial ventures in nearby towns.

Next to Patidars come Momens (Muslims) and Momins (Ismailis). Like the Chaudhuries they too are well known for their skill and care in maintaining milch animals. But unlike the Chaudhuries these two groups have sought to commercialize the milch animal trade. Both these groups have strong links with district salesmen, transport owners (for trucking the animals outside the district), and with various *tabelas* (cowsheds) in the city of Bombay.

Both of them bring to bear a commercial mentality to dairying and are therefore not very popular with the dairying community of the district which believes that they are responsible for exporting some of the vital animal resource of the region. We shall illustrate the approach of the Momens by taking the example of a village called

Kakoshi, and the operations of the Momins by taking the illustration of a village called Methan.

After that we shall take into account a village called Boratwada, which has a mixed population dominated by a cross-section of economically backward social groups. Nevertheless, by extending the principle of cooperative organization to many sectors of its economic life, the people of Boratwada have tried very hard to escape their own grinding poverty.

Pamol

Pamol is a typical Chaudhury village which did not want to be left behind the Patidar dominated villages in the district as far as its own economic development was concerned. Its advancement was due, essentially, to the hardworking nature of the Chaudhuries, their leadership, the extraordinary skill of their womenfolk in keeping the milch animals, their own social cohesion and, above all, a vying relationship with Patidars in matters of economic development. For the Chaudhuries, Pamol was indeed a shining example of what they could achieve once they put their minds to it.

The fact that the founding father of Dudhsagar, Mansinhbhai Patel (Patel in this case was not a caste surname but referred to the village headmanship or Patelship enjoyed by his family in the past), was a Chaudhury, had electrified his own people throughout the district. They on their part promised him their fullest cooperation whenever he approached them.

In 1966, Mansinhbhai visited Pamol and asked, in particular, a highly successful Chaudhury milk trader in the village to help him organize a milk cooperative. Milk traders, all over India, are totally opposed to milk cooperatives. In fact the principal aim of any milk cooperative is to eliminate the milk trader. The Pamol milk trader, who was thus approached, namely, Rambhai Chaudhury, had a flourishing business of his own. He, however, found Mansinhbhai's appeal irresistible. After that in less than two decades he, Rambhai, made Pamol an outstanding success in dairy cooperatives.

The village already had good milch animals. Moreover, the Chaudhury women had brought those animals to their maximum milk-giving capability. The quality of these had been further improved with the help of the artificial insemination programme and balanced feed provided by the Dudhsagar dairy. In the shortest possible time, an already prosperous village came to have a booming milk economy.

By 1989, Pamol, a village of 6000 people, had an income from the sale of milk which was about Rs11.7m and was growing at the rate of more than Rs1m a year.

Its agricultural income, which was roughly Rs5.5m in the same year, had almost reached a saturation point and was not registering much progress. Moreover, its income from milk had helped in injecting the necessary liquidity in its agricultural economy. Such a liquidity had helped the farmers to convert the bulk of their transactions from credit to cash. They could now buy better seeds, more fertilizers and pesticide, and also employ more agricultural labourers during peak seasons.

The availability of supplementary cash also helped farmers to switch to cash crops such as cotton, mustard, castor, tobacco and potatoes. But in that respect they had also reached an optimum from their agricultural income. At the other extreme dairying, especially with the help of high yielding cross-bred cows, held out a good many possibilities for increasing their income. Consequently, the milk producing community of Pamol started switching in a big way to the cross-bred cows. Pamol's milk economy, as compared to other villages, was thus on the road to becoming one of the mega milk economies of rural India.

Pamol, however, had its own economically depressed segments too. These consisted of certain sections of the Harijan and Adivasi communities. They were, by and large, the landless. Consequently they could not afford to keep milch animals. To that extent they were left out of the mainstream of economic development which had benefited the other segments of society. Both these groups had depended generally on agricultural labour. With the phenomenal growth of the agricultural economy, they did get work for more than six months in a year, locally. Moreover, in the peak season there was always a shortage of labour. Consequently their daily wages, especially during those periods, also went up.

But the enlightened leadership of Pamol wanted to do something special for its own poor. It therefore obtained permission to convert a part of its barren *gauchar* (village common) into a cooperative fodder farm. In three years it converted the fodder farm into a lush green patch, protected on all sides by several rows of tall eucalyptus trees. The farm then provided grass to the poor, at a reasonable rate, so that they could now keep a milch animal without any agricultural land of their own. Moreover, it also provided a number of agricultural labourers with year-round employment. Various banks in the district, because of the effective intervention of the milk cooperatives, could now give loans to the poor, along with a subsidy. And surprisingly, most of the loan takers also paid back their loans in the shortest possible time.

While the economic condition of the poor and the very poor had marginally improved, that of the better off, because of the favourable turns in both agricultural and dairy developments, had substantially improved. The net result of this, therefore, was a further widening of the existing economic disparity.

Bapupura

The milk economy of Bapupura, a village of over 2000 people, has become in recent years another mega milk economy and consequently a show place of the district along with Pamol. The village is predominantly inhabited by the Chaudhury caste, the well-known breeders of milch animals. The rest of the castes consisted of potters, carpenters, Harijans and tribals. Since its agricultural land is limited from all sides, with neighbouring villages unwilling to sell their land, the inhabitants of Bapupura were forced to seek their economic development either through dairying or by going out into the neighbouring town of Mansa. They chose to do both.

The milk scene of the village started changing in the early 1980s when cross-bred cows hit the scene. Like the Chaudhuries of Pamol, in the earlier phase of dairying, they too had vastly improved the milk yield of their *mehsani* buffalo but there was a limit to its productivity. When cross-bred cows became increasingly available, the Chaudhuries swiftly replaced their milk herd with it. Some of those cows gave more than 40 litres of milk per day and had to be milked four times during twenty-four hours, including once at midnight. And while the Chaudhury women complained about the extra work which such an animal had created for them, and especially about their aching fingers, they were also happy to see the increased cash come into the household. Bapupura sent 5000 litres of milk to Dudhsagar per day (1985–86), and its milk coop brought into the village Rs4.5m. This meant that the village was earning Rs2000 per person per year from milk alone. That indeed was a remarkable achievement for a village which was one-third the size of the highly prestigious village of Pamol. That income, however, leapt to Rs7.6m in 1989.

Such an increased liquidity enabled some of the economically ambitious Chaudhuries to start commercial ventures in the nearby town of Mansa. One of the Chaudhury families for instance made Rs46,000 from milk in one year, and helped one of its members to start a *pedhi* (commission agency) in Mansa. His family did not give up residence in Bapupura; it stayed there, looked after land and cowshed, and commuted by bus several times a week. The family thus diversified and increased its sources of income. Similarly there were others who started cloth stores, stores for medical supplies, groceries, electrical goods, transistors, etc.

Bapupura had also developed an internal credit system for its milk producers. Routinely, its milk coop gave 20 loans per year to its various members to increase the size of their herd. On top of that it also helped secure loans for its members from banks. So then in the expansion of the milk resource of the village, not only were there individual efforts but also more institutional ones.

The bulk of its milk producers owned land ranging from two to five acres. They lived in houses with brick walls and often with tiles on the roof and relatively more expensive furniture and gadgets inside, and even had walled courtyards.

Bapupura, nevertheless, had its own blind spot. As a village it had done very little for its poor. While it gave about the best wage in the district to its landless labourers (Rs15 per day to a male worker), and a *bharo* of farm cuttings, it was not actively involved, until recently, in arranging loans for milch animals for its poor. During the last two years the top executives and vets of Dudhsagar persuaded it to help its poor over and above the possibility of getting loans from the bank. Since the bulk of its milk producers were switching to cross-bred cows, their discarded *mehsanis* were increasingly becoming available to the poor of the village, sometimes at very reasonable rates. Then there was the direct intervention of the vet who routinely targeted some of the poor families of the village for an indigenous cow and a cross-bred female calf. Such provisions together with the availability of *bharo* was just about slowly beginning to change the condition of the poor in the village. Nevertheless, the fact remained that the arrival of the cross-bred cows had further widened the income disparity in the community. While the wages of the poor increased marginally, the income of their employers has more than doubled since the arrival of the new animal.

Gagaret

Gagaret is a Patidar village which has been in the forefront of economic prosperity. This it was able to achieve by means of a diversified approach to its economic resources and potential. It paid equal attention to agriculture and dairying in the village, and when individuals within its families were ready to start commercial ventures, and in some cases small manufacturing units, they moved to the nearby small towns. Those who moved out maintained strong ties with the rest of the family and vice-versa.

Although not the best keepers of the animals in the district, the Patidars of Gagaret have continued to search for the most efficient animal. In its various gossip-groups there is an ongoing businesslike discussion on how to make their animals more efficient in terms of cost and benefit. As a community, therefore, it has been most receptive to experimenting both with cattle feed and artificial insemination. And whatever is fed, and inseminated, immediately becomes an item in the gossip circuit. Within the village one therefore sees the most efficient buffaloes and cross-bred cows. Individuals within the village collect district-wide information on the productivity of certain animals and what in fact led to it. They then feed the same to the local gossip circuits and then enter into a lively demand-response debate with the visiting vet. They nag him and challenge him to give them equally productive animals.

To most of them the search for the most efficient animals comes as a personal challenge as well as a matter of economic benefit. A senior vet at Dudhsagar once stated that he had never seen so much enthusiasm on the part of men and women for an efficient animal, bordering on a craze, as in Gagaret.

For the Patidars, the search for the most productive and efficient animals, in terms of cost-benefit, is a part of their wider search and thrust towards economic development. With them, however, there are no deep personal attachments to the animals as in the case of the Chaudhury women. In Gagaret you do not hear the word *mamta* or *athwar* towards the animal as you hear in Pamol. It is the milk, its quantity and fat content, that most people are concerned with.

Their supplementary income from milk has helped the Patidars of Gagaret to have more and more bore wells for their farms either cooperatively with the owners of their neighbouring fields or jointly with their relatives. Moreover, to them the income from milk, although in small amounts but far more frequent and readily available, proves very handy for buying seeds, fertilizers and pesticides, whenever these become available on short notice. Such an income has therefore proved to be very helpful for a variety of inputs they need for their agriculture.

The Patidars of Gagaret have also turned the village into a thriving market for cross-bred cows. They either buy and sell those cows or keep elaborate information on villages which want to buy or sell them, take their customers there and then charge them commission. In that process they used to bring cross-bred cows from Bapupura. And now Bapupura also wants to get into the business. All these developments are so very recent (1987), that their impact on the community could not be fully assessed.

In recent years a number of Patidars have tried their hand at commercial ventures. In the district of Mehsana we may be witnessing a repeat performance of what happened in the Kaira district. In Kaira district, cooperative dairying first of all gave an additional stimulus to its agricultural economy and then helped in providing, to some extent, the much needed liquidity in starting commercial and industrial ventures.

But in that respect Kaira district had some advantages of its own. For one thing it has been blessed with very good soil, water facilities, and the hardworking and enterprising community of Leva Patidars. Moreover, cooperative dairying there is now nearly four decades old. These together gave Kaira a headstart over the economy of other districts.

Mehsana Patidars secretly admire the achievements of Kaira Patidars for their energy and progress in agriculture, commerce, and now in industry. Without admitting to outsiders, they find themselves running in a race, while being in an emulative relationship with their counterparts across the district divide so as to be able to shorten the time-span for attaining what the others have already achieved. And for a student of society this is indeed a fascinating process to watch.

Kakoshi

Kakoshi is a large village. In 1985, its population was estimated to be above 7000. It has a very poor access road from the highway. And during heavy monsoon seasons, access to it is difficult. The relative inaccessibility of Kakoshi, from its neighbouring villages, has given it a distinct flavour and identity of its own. It has a large population of Momens who have retained their distinct Gujarati Muslim identity since the days of Muslim rulers in the region centuries ago. The brightly lit shops and merchandise, restaurants (and there are far too many of those) and dresses makes one feel that Kakoshi is not a part of rural Mehsana.

The population of Kakoshi consists mainly of Momens (nearly 50 per cent), Thakores, Rabaris, Prajapatis, Panchals and Harijans. Besides these there are a few families of Brahmins, Banias, Patidars and Sonis who have come from outside. The Momens are considered to be a very hardworking community. In agriculture, dairying, milch animals trade, commercial ventures, etc., they have done exceedingly well.

For a long time, the Momens of Kakoshi have been exporting the *mehsani* to various cattle markets of India and, in particular, to the *tabelawalas* (cowshed owners) of Bombay. Earlier that trade was controlled by the Patidars. But the Momens got an edge over them by means of their control over the transportation system, and also by posting their own men in various markets.

Practically every evening, heavy trucks loaded with six to nine *mehsanis* go to the city of Bombay, deposit the high milk yielding animal there and bring back those which require artificial insemination, or need to be sent away to slaughter houses. The traders, who bring back near dry animals from Bombay, expect the Dudhsagar vets to revive their milk giving capacity. The vets for their part keep on complaining, but so far they have not succeeded in stopping the practice. Although there is a government ban of some sort on exporting animals across the state borders it has not been very effective.

Besides a flourishing milch animals trade, Kakoshi also has an active milk cooperative society which was established in 1970. Before that the milk producers sold milk to the local market or made *ghee* (purified butter) from it.

The Momens are deeply involved in making their milk cooperative a success. For one thing, their milch animal trade required them to send out animals, which were first of all tried out in the village itself. Such an imperative also indirectly helped the village milk cooperative. What followed was simply incredible. Unlike most other village cooperatives, where women usually line up with tiny brass or stainless steel vessels or small aluminium cans, the women of Kakoshi bring milk in *charus* (vessels for drinking water) or big plastic buckets.

Since Kakoshi is well known for its high-yielding animals, it is very rare that you see women using smaller vessels to carry milk to the collection centre.

What is missing in the Kakoshi scene is the big number of cross-bred cows. That has yet to hit the commercial side of the milch animal trade. Chances are the rich *tabelawalas* of the city of Bombay, who are always short of room for their cowsheds, will grab this high-yielding animal. They will in turn expect a village like Kakoshi to switch from buffaloes to cross-bred cows. That in turn will not only push up the already high price of cross-bred cows but also result in the neglect of buffaloes as the principal milch animal which the poorer sections of society can afford. The dynamics of that shift, with their social consequences on the community as a whole, can only be examined when they actually unfold.

Methan

Methan has a population of 3200 (1984), out of which more than two-thirds are Momin Ismailis, the devout followers of the Aga Khan. The rest of the village consists of Thakores, Rabaris, Praja-patis, Harijans, etc.

Methan is a unique village. Its closely knit, well-educated Ismaili population, with a highly developed commercial sense, gives it a character of its own. Since it is also integrally connected with Momin Ismaili *tabelawalas* of Bombay, it appears as a commercial outpost of a distant people in the heart of rural Mehsana. Its rich buffalo merchants – whose livelihood it is to go on sending good milch animals to Bombay and in return receive enormous amounts of money – appear to be more deeply rooted in their own ethnic community, and in the commercial enterprise that it is engaged in, rather than in the wider human community within which it is located. It is also one of the few villages in the district which looks at milk cooperatives from the perspective of a commercial people rather than through the wider goals of the district, and its variety of people, that such a cooperative organization serves. No matter when you go there, the village always clamours for a better price for milk from the cooperative. Methan developed itself into a flourishing milch animal export centre long before a milk cooperative was established there. Nearly 50 years ago it established its Bombay connection and has steadily expanded it ever since. Some of the traders in it also have their own transport trucks which helps their trade.

Apart from the steady income which they earn from milk, while the high milk yielding animal is being groomed for the Bombay market, the advantage of their membership lies in facilities which the cooperative provides in reviving the animals which return from Bombay's *tabelas*. The returned animals, to say the least, are always in bad shape and place an undue burden on the vets and the shareholders of the Dudhsagar dairy in general.

However, there is another side to Methan village. The Momin Ismailis have also done a lot of social work in the village. They have established a well-equipped hospital, schools, and an enormous *gobar* (bio) gas plant for the entire village. This plant is now run by the women of the village.

Boratwada

Boratwada is one of the less-developed villages of Mehsana. This was due to its extremely poor soil, proximity to a big town called Harij, which monopolized all the developmental resources of the sub-district, and a cross-section of population lacking in entrepreneurial spirit. Therefore, for a long time the village did not attract the attention of social workers or politicians. Finally, in the 1950s and early 1960s it developed its own leadership and from then on things began to change within the village. Simultaneously, it also received the attention of various bodies at the district level.

The leading spirit of the village was Karsanbhai Chaudhury. He, like Mansinhbhai, the founding father of the Dudhsagar dairy, came under the influence of Mahatma Gandhi's emphasis on the need to work for rural upliftment. After independence he therefore plunged into social work in his own village and its surrounding areas. As could be expected, he started with schools and built some of the finest educational institutions in the area, the faculty of which has won national awards.

One of his greatest achievements was the establishment of a group of cooperative societies in the village. First, he established a *Seva Society* in 1961. It provided its members with seeds, fertilizers and consumer items such as sugar, edible oil, *ghee*, soap, matches and whatever else the members asked for. This was then followed, in 1964, by a cooperative society for sharing water from bore wells called the *Khedut Piyat Society*. In 1989 the village had six cooperatively run bore wells. The village milk cooperative society was established in 1965.

The establishment of various cooperative societies in the village, as early as the middle 1960s, changed the outlook of the villagers. Despite a mixed population of Chaudhuries, Rabaris, Thakardas, Rawals, Harijans, etc., with very little education and ability to come together and work together in the past, the village through its own cooperative organizations became a highly efficient operative unit.

In 1976 it appointed a committee for loans to be given to the poor for which provision was already made by the state government. But the officials of the bank, who were supposed to provide the loans, were not always willing to act. Under pressure from the committee not only were the loans provided for buying milch animals, but they were also recovered from the individuals who had borrowed the money.

In 1983 the village had embarked on yet another ambitious programme of having a cooperatively owned and managed fodder farm, similar to the one in Pamol. This would then help the landless to buy hay and lucerne grass from the fodder farm at a reasonable rate, in certain months in a year, and be able to maintain milch animals.

Boratwada was possibly the only village in the district which persuaded women to become active members of various cooperative committees. Consequently, very often two-thirds of the membership of various committees consisted of women, and highly vocal ones at that. And what is more, despite their initial hesitations and conventional inhibitions, they all worked in mixed female-male situations.

While Boratwada did not make stunning progress, economically, as its own agricultural and animal resources were limited, nevertheless, from 1960 onwards it had become, in a genuine sense, a self-governing community. It sought to resolve all its social problems by means of a cooperative effort. In doing so it earned the respect of a lot of other rural communities in the district. In a sense it was imbued by the same spirit, at the village level, which had inspired Dudhsagar, and its organizers, at the district level. And in doing so it found its own escape from the grinding poverty of centuries.

Irana

The district of Mehsana came to have its first all-women milk coop by accident rather than design. Originally its milk cooperative was established in 1971, but soon fights developed between and within its various ethnic groups leading to its closure. When it was reopened, after a lapse of a few years, it gave, to everyone's surprise, an extraordinary account of itself. For the second time around not men but women were solely in charge of the rejuvenated institution.

The village of Irana is close to the rapidly industrialising town of Kadi. Kadi is nationally acknowledged as the centre for the pharmaceutical industry and, within the state, as a centre of ceramics. Irana's proximity to an urban centre meant that it was subject to raids from milk traders who wanted to break its coop at any cost. Towards such a breakage the ethnic cleavages and family fights within the village were most helpful.

The population of Irana consists of over 450 households, more than 100 of which belong to Rajputs (Vaghelas and Jadejas), 90 to Thakores (Kshatriyas), 45 to Rabaris (Desais), 80 to Harijans (Venkars), and the rest to economically and socially backward castes. The Rabaris of Irana in the past not only controlled its milk coop but also kept a private milk business going with the help of traders from Kadi. Since they were used to mixing water with milk, they increasingly came in conflict with the officials of Dudhsagar. Later on two prosperous Rabari brothers fought in the village and this forced Dudhsagar to close down the milk coop. The villagers were so much terrorised by them that they dared not oppose such a move. After its closure, the Rabaris wanted the milk production of the village to go to Kadi through them. For some time the villagers put up with it. Later on the women of the village approached a women's social work organization called *Matrudham* in the city of Ahmedbad with a view to reviving the milk coop, this time to be managed entirely by the women of the village. Dudhsagar, which was now increasingly concentrating on women, readily agreed to the proposal.

Initially, the Rabaris, with the help of traders, tried to harass the women, but the latter remained firm. Moreover, since there were women from most of the ethnic groups of the village, including the families of those Rabaris, their threats were not taken seriously. Finally, since the support of Dudhsagar was there, in most unmistakable terms, the Rabaris began to back off.

Within two years of its revival not only did Irana's milk collection phenomenally increase but its fat content was considered to be one of the highest in the district. During those two years, women were also able to enroll 105 members from nearly a quarter of the households of the village. And on its executive committee there were women from a cross-section of the community, including Harijans, presided over by a Rajput woman and assisted by a Brahmin woman secretary.

Irana's milk coop, from day one of its restart in 1979, had a pro-woman and pro-poor bias. Since the men of the village had demonstrated their inability to look after the coop, they had no other alternative but to put up with the gender shift that had occurred in its management. But they were confident that women would not be able to run it for long, and then they would get in. Women on their part worked very hard, and as a team, so as not to fail in the face of men's malicious predictions. By 1987 they were going from strength to strength, making plans for a building of their own and a very ambitious plan for animal health care and artificial insemination. Even the vets and top organizers of Dudhsagar were deeply involved in the success of the women in Irana. Moreover, they were also hopeful that the women would be able to pay much more attention to the poor of the village and make it *their* responsibility to help them get loans.

By 1987 we could also observe that the gender rivalry for the control of the milk coop had also gone into the background. What had emerged in its place was a village-wide watchfulness towards the possible attempts by the milk traders, and their agents inside the village, to break the organization, if necessary by dividing women themselves. In 1989 such attempts were being made to break their unity.

The various developments in Irana were thus far too recent to be able to observe changes resulting therefrom. Nevertheless, what it reflected was a major shift in the concentration of Dudhsagar: from men to women; and from productivity to the inclusion of the poor in their enterprise.

SOME CONCLUDING OBSERVATIONS

As we saw in the preceding pages, Dudhsagar has successfully acted as a catalyst in the rural development of the district of Mehsana which has had a number of natural limitations. What it has provided to the district is the much needed income to various segments of its population. It has been able to achieve this for all those strata of society which have some land no matter how very small. Moreover, in a number of cases it has also been able to provide such an income to some of its landless, and, more specifically, to those among them who, along with their wages, are able to get a *bharo*. In fact, barring certain months of the year, this is the most common practice in most villages of the district.

Then there are villages like Pamol and Boratwada, where an extraordinary attempt has been made to convert a part of the *gauchar* land (village common) into a cooperative fodder farm especially for those who are landless and therefore unable to take advantage of loans to buy milch animals. There are at the moment only a few examples of this in the district, nevertheless, this new idea is likely to become increasingly popular.

Moreover, it has also provided the much-needed cash to be able to change the operations of agricultural economy from credit to cash. In other words, it has injected into the economic transactions, and economic relationships in general, some amount of liquid cash. In fact the inhabitants of so many villages claimed that there is now a decline in the per capita debt in rural communities. That, however, needs to be checked.

The average farmer, with provision for extra cash, is now in a position to employ more labourers on his farm. What is more, that extra cash, which comes in three times a month, and which is not subject to the vagaries of the market, has the potential of being spent as it comes in. For it is not like the money which can come in only when the crop is ready, cut and sold in the market after an interval of roughly four months. As opposed to that the dairy cash is steady and readily available cash, albeit for small uses. It can be spent as it comes in.

A large number of farmers receive on an average Rs100 to Rs150 a month by way of their income from milk. Such an income proves to be most handy, even for the most prosperous among them, to buy a few bags of fertilizer or pesticide – which are always in short supply – when they suddenly come onto the market.

A number of farmers claimed that they use those small amounts for minor purposes on the farm. By way of illustration they repeatedly mentioned the levelling up of land at the edges or getting good top soil evenly spread before the next round of cultivation. Consequently, with the help of the extra cash not only have they brought more land under cultivation but have also qualitatively improved it.

The milk cooperative, despite its best intentions, has not been able to reach all those who are desperately poor in rural communities and therefore could do precious little with the help of the organizational muscle which it has developed. This is particularly true of certain segments of the Harijan and Adivasi communities. For centuries some of them have lived as marginal people who received only what they were offered, rather than demanded what they thought they deserved. Consequently most of them, particularly in recent years, do not come to know what has been provided for them by way of public policy. They also do not know what they could get by organizing themselves for their own advancement.

Within the district there are a few shining examples such as Boratwada where the local leadership systematically went after bureaucrats and politicians to give them what had been provided by way of public policy. But not all the rural communities in the district have such enlightened leadership.

The cooperative dairies cannot pressure district banks to give loans to the poor or give subsidies to them to buy milch animals despite the fact that provision for this has been made in most regions. For that the leadership has to come from the local community. Moreover, it cannot always persuade the bureaucracy to help convert various *gauchars* into cooperative fodder farms. In that respect its hands would be very much strengthened if it were to receive help from urban intellectuals, rural social workers and all those who cry out for social justice but do not want to do anything about it in practical terms.

Then there is the serious problem of further widening the income disparity, even more than what it already is, by means of an accelerated growth in the economic development of the district. In the past such disparities were widened in various rural communities of India by measures such as irrigation, the introduction of cash crops, and the Green Revolution in general. These substantially improved the economic condition of the better-off segments of rural society rather than that of the poorer sections. A similar threat seems to have presented itself with the introduction of the cross-bred cows. Since they cost nearly three times as much as a *mehsani*, only the better-off sections of the rural population will be able to afford them. And so far as their milk yield is concerned it is proportionately far greater. Moreover, the cost of maintaining such an animal is much less than that of an average *mehsani*. Consequently, like the earlier measures to accelerate economic development, the cross-bred cows as well would widen the income disparity within the rural communities.

This does present a cruel dilemma. While an efficient dairy development requires the introduction of the most efficient animal, in doing so you also worsen one of your toughest problems, namely, that of income disparity.

In Pamol, for instance, there are farmers who have been able to double or even triple their income from milk in the last two years by investing in cross-bred cows. Whereas the wages which they have paid to landless workers even in the peak agricultural seasons have not gone up by more than twenty-five percent (from Rs12 to Rs15) in 1989.

The presence of such a dilemma therefore means that the planners and developers of rural India will have to do something exclusive for the poorer sections of the rural population. They will have to help these segments develop special skills, by means of an ambitious affirmative programme, which can help them to catch up with the others. There is no such thing in the offing at the moment. Moreover, this will require a concerted effort on the part of all those bodies which are engaged in developing rural areas.

To conclude, the achievements of Dudhsagar in developing a backward district like Mehsana were very many. Not only had it stimulated the growth of its rural economy but it had also set in motion the economic development of its various emerging towns. Moreover, it had significantly improved upon its greatest resource, namely the *mehsani*, and was also engaged in improving the milk yield of its cross-bred cows. Such a resource together with the care and skill of its milk-producing community in maintaining milch animals, will make Dudhsagar the greatest milk cooperative of India before long.

Moreover, in recent years the management of Dudhsagar and its vets, right down the line, have taken it upon themselves to target the poor of each rural community for development. They have first of all maintained detailed records of what is happening in those communities. Then they have begun to pressure those communities to look after the poor as part of the community's responsibility. But they, the organizers, have not stopped there. They frequently visit those villages, call meetings, put pressure on the chairmen and secretaries, promise rewards of special attention and then see to it that those communities also get involved in helping their poor. Moreover, its organizers get directly involved in pressuring villages to help their resourceless widows by approaching banks and various welfare agencies for loans for milch animals for them. They are also constantly pressuring the state-level bureaucrats and politicians to help them start more and more cooperatively owned and run fodder farms for the poor of the village.[3] Finally, the vets in particular make a list of households for giving away indigenous cows with a cross-bred female calf. Dudhsagar's senior vets and executives in particular are deeply involved in making such a resource available to the poor of various rural communities.

The years of 1984, 1985 and 1986 were the years of terrible drought in certain sub-districts of Mehsana. During those years, Dudhsagar targeted 40 worst affected villages and started supplying them with buttermilk for their poor. It sent double concentrates of buttermilk to those villages each day, so that it could be diluted by the recipient and stretched through the day. Such a relief cargo went out to the poor, day after day, earning their deep gratitude. Dudhsagar's effort also attracted an inordinately large number of voluntary agencies (33), and they too pitched in a variety of ways to avert the loss of life and animals through those terrible years in rural Mehsana.[4]

While this generation of Dudhsagar's organizers is deeply involved in the poor of the district, it remains to be seen how far the next generation would continue those traditions.

3 Sumul Dairy: a milk cooperative of the deprived

Sumul dairy, in the city of Surat in south Gujarat, represents a fascinating example of a shift in the nature and composition of a milk cooperative. Started as an organisation of milk traders, Sumul initially became a cooperative of people with a sizeable landholding and ended up as an institution which was heavily based among the Adivasis or the tribals of the district. The Adivasis have either poor quality land or no land at all. In 1983–84 the organizers of Sumul proudly reported that 73.6 per cent of its total milk collection of 44,020,620 litres, came from the district's tribal village.[1] That was indeed a remarkable achievement by any standard. Sumul, it was evident, had succeeded in inducting the Adivasis within the framework of a common economic organisation and thereby had furnished them with new economic and political opportunities in the district.

The district of Surat has 13 talukas or sub-districts, and out of those nine are predominantly tribal. For a long time, and almost continuously in recent years, the Adivasis have been a source of cheap labour both in the rural and urban communities of the district. Moreover, both the urban dwellers and rural communities were so very used to the domestic help and farm labour offered by the Adivasis that they had consistently discouraged and opposed any effort at improving their economic condition.

Through a succession of economic changes within the district, by means of irrigation, different cash crops, expanding markets for vegetables and fruit, sugar cane, etc., the condition of the landless labourers among the Adivasis had not materially changed. They had no doubt received higher wages and for more days in a year, nevertheless, the condition of the farm workers among them had not significantly improved.

Even those with land among them, being cut off from the mainstream of economic life of society, did not do very well. Apart from the poor quality of their land, their own insulation from various changes, information regarding new seeds and agricultural techniques and lack of access to the newly-created resources and opportunities for the farmers, acted as major constraints on their economic development.

Sumul's penetration into such communities, as we shall presently see, was not easy. Apart from the sheer logistics of reaching out to them, in the absence of transport and communication facilities, the major problem was that of creating the very culture of milk, and dairying, where none existed before. A large number of Adivasi communities were not habituated to drinking milk. In some of those communities neither men nor women knew how to milk milch animals. Then there were problems relating to animal care and of considering dairying as such an auxiliary means to economic development. Finally, there were the problems relating to the organization of the structure of the milk cooperative and book-keeping which were by no means easy for the uninitiated. To convert a non-dairy community into a milk-producing community required, in short, a lot of dedication, commitment, effort and patience on the part of the organisers of Sumul.

But before Sumul could move in that direction, it had to disengage itself from its early involvement with the trader class and start paying more attention to the people who needed its help the most, namely the Adivasis. Such a major shift in policy was not easy to sell to those in its apex body who had their own vested interests to serve.

In the hierarchically ordered social organization of India, different ethnic groups, with their economic bases, and social advantages and disadvantages, manifested a differing range of ability to benefit by various new economic opportunities. Their differentiated response, either to such opportunities or to planned development stimulus in general, created a special problem for certain social groups within the traditional hierarchy. Those at the top of the social organisation often grabbed, or even monitored, new opportunities and provisions from which they could benefit in a widespread culture of development; those in the middle, either by way of envy or emulation, also benefited, in course of time, by making use of a part of those opportunities; but those at the base needed special effort at mobilization before they could be prepared to get anything out of what was ostensibly earmarked for them. In the absence of such a mobilization, and that is more often a rule than exception, very little by way of development effort reached the lowest strata of Indian society.

A similar response was there to the opportunities created in the district by cooperative dairying. Its first beneficiaries were those who, in relative terms, needed it the least. And those who needed it the most waited for a prior mobilization to prepare them for such an opportunity. Such a mobilization, as we shall see, came through a variety of sources, leaving behind an imprint of its own on the community they mobilized. Consequently, a number of communities where such efforts were made did not come forth with a uniform response.

This chapter is divided into four parts: background and orientation of Sumul; variety of mobilization efforts; some rural communities; and some general observations. We shall now examine each of them in some detail.

BACKGROUND AND ORIENTATION OF SUMUL

The milk cooperative movement of Surat had itself benefited enormously as a result of the experience gained in building previous cooperatives in different segments of its economy. As early as 1928, Sardar Patel, while preparing the Bardoli sub-district for the well-known *Bardoli Satyagraha* against the alien rule, had exhorted the farmers to build cooperative organisations and transact their economic business through them. From his point of view the middlemen could neither be trusted economically nor politically. His exhortations had resulted in the formation of some of the earliest coops in the district in the field of cotton ginning and pressing. Then, in 1939, an attempt was made to establish a cooperative in the city of Surat to collect milk from villages and then distribute it in the city itself. Such an attempt did not confine itself to milk only. It also included fruits and vegetables. In the course of time more and more such organisations came into existence, competed with one another, and then either amalgamated or disappeared.

The person who brought the various cooperatives under one umbrella and gave them a comprehensive structure was Jagjivandas Patel, popularly known as Daskaka. Nationalist leaders such as Sardar Patel and Morarji Desai, who were directly involved in building Amul dairy in 1946, suggested that Daskaka should also build such an organisation for Surat district. Finally, after a series of meetings to iron out differences among the leading politicians of the district, some of whom had their own pocket borough style coops, in 1951 it was decided to amalgamate the existing bodies under a new organisation called Sumul.

Initially Sumul was a cooperative of milk collectors and traders rather than of producers. Later on, when some milk producers tried to send milk directly to Sumul, the collectors and traders deeply resented it. Consequently, in order to teach a lesson to Sumul, for bypassing them, they came out in direct competition against it. Instead of sending their own collection to Sumul, as per earlier undertakings, they started sending it directly to the consumers in Surat. As opposed to Sumul's delivery of milk at predesignated stalls, the collectors and traders made home delivery to consumers. However, their hope of breaking up Sumul, an organisation they had supported earlier, proved futile, and a short time later they disappeared from the milk economy.

By 1968, Sumul acquired the look of a modern dairy, with its own regular collection of milk, pasteurisation plant, and a reliable distribution system. In 1970 it introduced the system of payment based on fat content, and provided the necessary equipment for measuring it to its village milk cooperatives. Given the sprawling character of the city of Surat, it had to keep an eye on the milk traders who wanted to raid its sources of milk collection in various peri-urban villages and break their cooperative organisations.

In the early 1970s, in search of an increased supply of milk, which was in great demand in the burgeoning commercial and industrial city of Surat, Sumul had started exploring the possibility of building cooperative societies in its tribal villages. It was indeed a bold move. For one thing, most of those villages had neither milch animals nor the necessary experience of looking after them. As stated earlier, a number of them did not even have the habit of consuming milk. Sumul, therefore, came to realize that in such communities it would have to begin with ground zero; that before animals were brought in, what those communities needed was a demonstration in animal maintenance, milking and health care in general. Among other things what it did was to employ Rabari (the traditional keepers of animals) women to teach tribal women how to look after the animals and milk them. During such milking exercises, some of the tribal women used to complain of pain in their untrained thumbs and fingers. Then there had to be lessons in book-keeping, maintaining records, and organizational matters in general. Initially the organizers of Sumul used to depend on local leadership, social workers and missionaries. Later on they started covering one village after another with the help of their own veterinary staff. More about this later.

In reaching out to the tribals, Sumul was also faced with the problem of the inaccessibility of their villages. Most of them neither had access roads for the trucks to come and collect milk nor a concentrated residential area which could be regarded as the centre of the village.

Since most of the Adivasi villages were either on the periphery of forests or on hilly tracts, they, till recently, did not have roads on which the contractors of various transport companies would agree to run their vehicles. Consequently, a number of such villages had to bring their milk collection, twice a day, to the highway itself. As more approach roads were built by the state authority, more Adivasi villages became accessible, and the more they joined the cooperative organization of Sumul. But such an undertaking by the state authority was very slow indeed. Since the Adivasis did not have much political clout, excepting before elections, the amount budgeted for road construction in their region was rarely spent on time or with good results.

Then unlike most caste villages, the bulk of tribal villages did not have a concentrated *gamtham* or residential area. And in most of them it was often difficult to locate what may be regarded as the centre of the village. Only in recent years, have some of them got their primary schools and panchayat buildings. In such villages some kind of village centre has evolved. What finally reinforced the need for such a centre was the arrival of the milk cooperative society. Such a society at once became the centre of village activity. Not only that, most cooperatives also donated specific amounts to their own villages for the construction of a cooperative society building, a part of which could be used for community purposes. Then there were cases where coop money was donated towards the construction of waterworks in what subsequently became the centre of the village, access roads and veterinary units.

Despite the steady growth of the centre of activity in such villages, especially with the arrival of school, panchayat, milk coop, waterworks, etc., the established trend towards the decentralisation of the residential area could not be reversed in most tribal villages. Some Adivasis explained this by saying that traditionally, with death in the family, people either burnt down the hut in which someone had died or just deserted it and built a new one elsewhere in their fields. Such a practice compelled a constant residential movement with the result that most of them had moved around pretty well in all corners of their own land.

Before Sumul could link up distant Adivasi villages in different parts of the district, it had also to wait till its own chilling centres could be built in strategic areas so as to prevent the sourage of milk.

It was thus a bold move on the part of Sumul when it decided to bring in the Adivasi villages within its own cooperative structure. To be able to do that it had to attend to several problems, the most important of which was how to transform a people without means of dairying and even without the culture of using milk and milk products into a milk producing community.

Within the district itself dairying as an industry, first of all, developed in the sub-district of Olpad. Olpad has a population of Anavil Brahmins, Patidars, Koli Patels, Kshatriyas and Halpatis. Over the years large chunks of Anavil land had passed into the hands of Patidars. The Patidars, as a rule, got much more out of land, and whenever land came into the market, they were the first to bid for it. In Olpad the Patidars, and after them the Anavils, had entered into dairying in a big way. For both their economic undertakings, i.e. agriculture and dairying, they made use of the landless labourers, namely the Halpatis, and in recent years large groups of migrant farm workers from Maharastra, the neighbouring state.

After Olpad, dairying spread to the talukas of Kamrej, Palsana and Bardoli, with both Patidars and Anavils making use of the available landless labour. In some of the villages of these sub-districts, the organization of dairying had to be grouped together with the already existing cooperatives for fruits and vegetables. The notables among them were the Palsana Division Milk and Vegetable Marketing Cooperative, established in 1957, and the Umbhel Division Milk and Vegetable Growers Cooperative, established in 1968. Each of these divisions had several villages in them. Moreover, each of such villages also had a variety of consumer cooperatives.

Despite repeated efforts by the organizers of Sumul to reach out to the Halpatis in those villages, they could do precious little to get them into the expanding dairy industry. The landowning class of Patidars and Anavils, who controlled all the public institutions in the area, wanted a steady supply of cheap farm and domestic labour which the Halpatis provided. Consequently, they blocked all the efforts of Sumul to reach out to the Halpatis in those villages. The Patidars and Anavils rationalized their position by arguing that if Sumul helped the landless Halpatis to obtain milch animals, they would graze them in the fields of the former. In some of the premier agricultural talukas of the district, therefore, Sumul just could not get over the barrier erected by the landed vested interests in reaching out precisely to that segment of society which needed its help the most. The condition of Halpatis in villages not controlled by such a landed class, as we shall see later on, was different. In some of them the performance of Halpatis in dairying was about the best in the region.

At the district level, the same vested interests did not show much enthusiasm for Sumul's proposal to take dairying into Adivasi talukas. Such an effort, they thought, would deprive them of the control of decision-making bodies within Sumul in the long run. But their fears were misplaced. Despite a large proportion of Adivasi-membership of the cooperative dairy organization of Sumul, they have yet to generate their own leadership which would enter the sub-district and district level public bodies in a big enough way to be able to play an effective part in the democratic process of those organizations. So far there are isolated Adivasi leaders who then come under the influence of the district political bosses within the ruling party. Till the middle of the 1980s, the Adivasis were content with the economic benefits which the coop dairy had brought to their villages. On their part, therefore, there was the problem of percep-tion of the need and political capacity to participate effectively in the sub-district and district level public bodies.

VARIETY OF MOBILISATION EFFORTS

Let us now examine the variety of mobilization efforts to include various ethnic groups and rural communities into the milk coopera-tive organization.

As noted in the earlier section, some of the villages, especially in the Palsana and Umbhel regions, did not need any mobilization efforts. They were involved in cooperative dairying even before Sumul came into existence. What they needed, nevertheless, was an adaptation to the new organization of Sumul, on the one hand, and a basic change of attitude towards the economically poor, on the other. The latter was indeed slow to come by.

The Anavils and Patidars within the older organizations had learnt not only how to operate such bodies but also learnt to make use of it in defending their own economic interests by a skillful use of its democratic process. With such a well-developed political capacity, and a strong agricultural base of their own, they had steadily advanced on the economic scale ever looking for, and grabbing, all

the development opportunities that were created for the advancement of rural communities. They therefore did not need any further
mobilization. They had done inordinately well for themselves. What
they needed, on the other hand, was a framework of constraint which
might not discourage their economic advancement but also allow and
help others to come up.

Ironically enough all the development efforts also needed their
cooperation to be able to show impressive results in the shortest
possible time. For they were capable of producing their own leadership, organizational talent, relentless drive towards continual economic advancement, and results. The road to development then was
through the already developed.

The already developed set up the role model for the various social
segments economically, and traditionally, below them. There was
often a relationship of emulation between the Anavils, Patidars, and
Kshatriyas and other groups in those communities. In most of them
the Kshatriyas moved through envy and emulation of the groups
above them.

But social groups which needed help at mobilization and leadership
were the lower segments of village society often consisting of
traditionally lower castes, Harijans and Adivasis. Even when some of
them had small pieces of land, their economic advancement depended on the mobilization efforts of some social work minded
individuals and organizations to tell them what all was within their
reach, given all the development opportunities in contemporary rural
India. And if such efforts did not come forth, the development of
those lower social groups was then indefinitely delayed. In the
following pages we shall examine the variety of efforts made by
public policies, bureaucrats, missionaries, Gandhians, social
workers, vets, urbanised village youths, etc. to mobilize the socially
disadvantaged and economically backward segments of rural society
towards the latter's advancement. Such efforts, as we shall see, also
left behind the imprints of each on the communities they mobilized.

Since Indian independence there has been an extraordinary emphasis on the role of government in economic development and social
change in general. Jawaharlal Nehru was in a sense directly responsible for such an emphasis. It was also an integral part of his social
and political belief whereby state activity was seen as an indispensable activity in any fundamental social and economic transformation
of society. Having been denied the instrumentality of such an
activity, owing to India's political subjection by alien rulers for

centuries, it was natural for Nehru to view state institutions as great partners in social transformation. Consequently, during his regime, and also under his inspiration, subsequently, a large number of public institutions were created, planned development formulated and public policies towards social change in general introduced.

But very soon it became clear that those institutions, public policies, various social provisions and a gigantic bureaucracy could not by themselves produce the desired results; that what was missing in all this was a demanding and pressuring public; and that such a public could be created only by means of self-involvement and not by means of making it a receiver of what the bureaucracy and public institutions had to offer. One of Nehru's strongest critics in that respect was his comrade in the freedom struggle, namely Jayaprakash Narayan, popularly known as JP. He characterised Nehru's approach as governmentalism, where only the bureaucrats and corrupt politicians prospered.

Earlier, Mahatma Gandhi had emphasized the need for a massive social mobilization, and social and political involvement, by citizens of free India so as to bring about a basic change in social relationships by means of what he thought was the most effective means, i.e. self-involvement. For him, and after him for JP, the Indians had been a subject people for too long, and that had made them indifferent to what happened to their fellow beings. There was no short cut to self-development and a broader social change by means of self-involvement. Anything else would change neither the highly fossilized thinking and values of the Indians nor the network of their social relationships which favours only a few, both socially and economically. By involving themselves in the process of change not only will the Indians change their society but also themselves in a fundamental sense of the term.

In a sense the cooperative dairy movement in India represents an aspect of this controversy. Within its various attempts at mobilization there are emphases on a variety of agents of social change that we discussed in the foregoing pages. A number of states in India, which theoretically agree to launching milk cooperative organizations at the state, district and village levels, want overall control to be retained by the bureaucrats. They believe that milk cooperatives can be neither launched by a grass-roots movement nor sustained by it. For them whatever happened in various districts of Gujarat, and in a few other states, was something unique and was not likely to happen elsewhere. Needless to say such an attitude deprived the people of those states of a unique experience of building and operating their own economic institutions and thereby bringing about a change in their own thinking and social relationships in general.

So far as the politicization of the milk cooperative organization is concerned, the possibility of its being abused by electioneering politicians continually exists. As in the case of the Amul and Sabar dairies, politicians have always viewed, and will continue to view, the well-established network of cooperative organizations, going right down the village, as an enormous source of electoral support for themselves. Fortunately, so far these organizations, because of the watchful eye of several district level politicians, and also technocrats, have been prevented from out and out electoral exploitation.

What could not be prevented, however, was the involvement of politicians in distributing the benefits of Indira Gandhi's Twenty Point Programme during the period of the Emergency. The idea was to offer loans to the poor for buying milch animals. In a number of cases such loans went to deserving people. But in a large number of cases they went to people who could do without them. Moveover, a number of politicians also made huge financial gains and ensured continued electoral support for themselves.

To sum up this point, wherever public servants or politicians in charge of financial assistance got involved in the affairs of milk cooperatives, their involvement invariably produced adverse results. While the cooperative movement in Surat district, with all its heritage of voluntary activity since before independence, was a grass-roots movement, politicians' involvement in distributing funds under the Twenty Point Programme was a waste of public funds. Wherever loans under the programme were offered to the poor, without the interference of politicians and bureaucrats, the results were a little more favourable.

Christian missionaries have been working in tribal India for a long time. By and large their emphasis, as could be expected, has been on proselytizing the lower rungs of Indian society which had been neglected and condemned to indignities of all kinds by the caste system. In order to help the lower groups find an escape route from the inhumanities of the caste system, Christian missionaries have emphasized education, and the learning of trades, on the part of those whom they persuaded to embrace their faith. Most of the educational institutions run by them are so good that middle-class Indians from higher castes want their children to be educated by them.

In recent years, Christian missionaries have also started retraining themselves to be able to help their followers in the new ways of economic development. Some of them working in the Adivasi villages of Surat district even began taking training in how to organize a milk cooperative society. Under such a proposal, Father Gype, a Jesuit missionary from South India, belonging to a Spanish mission, took a course offered by the National Dairy Development Board, Anand, and then got down to the task of helping the Adivasis of a few villages to build their milk cooperatives. The organizers of Sumul were absolutely delighted in 1979 to see dairy-trained missionaries help them build milk cooperatives in remote Adivasi villages.

In the course of time Sumul's enthusiasm for the missionary run milk cooperatives began to wane. While such Adivasi villages had started prospering economically, with supplementary income from milk helping villagers to improve their standard of living, and even agriculture – as they could now buy better seeds and ferti- lizers – nevertheless, the missionaries maintained a rigid control on all the decision-making and thereby deprived the Adivasis of learning to manage their own institutions themselves. What the Adivasis were deprived of by missionary paternalism was an opportunity for self- development through self-involvement and all the operational lessons one learns through a process of trial-and-error. By 1982, Sumul's organizers were openly expressing concern over the external manage- ment of what was supposed to be a self-governing public institution, but they could do precious little.

There was, however, some difference in the styles of operation of the various missionaries in charge of overseeing the smooth running of the milk cooperatives. While the bulk of seven villages run by missionaries showed rigid paternalism, there was at least one where the clerical interference in lay matters was reduced to a minimum. In others there was too much anxiety expressed on behalf of the uninitiated Adivasis going wrong in running the public institution of milk cooperatives. The result was that barring the one uninterfered village, the Adivasis of the remaining six villages neither grew in their political capacity to manage their own public affairs democratically nor could they organizationally move forward, setting forth their own goals and lines of action. The paternalism of the missionaries, although well meant, had cost the Adivasis of six villages a measure of self-development on which one could not put any value. Especially in view of the fact that the Adivasis were denied scope for their own self-development almost since the dawn of Indian civilization, the treatment of them as wards and as undeveloped people had set their clock back once again.

The kind of leadership which Father Gype and his associates provided, by and large, created other-directed rather than self-directed organizations, to use Reisman's expression, which in the long run was bound to be resented by the Adivasis themselves. Moreover, a lot of their religious and economic activity was premised on an inadequate understanding of the highly complex cultural life of the Adivasis. In fact the Jesuit missionaries who had worked with them for more than a decade had confessed to us their inability to understand the way the Adivasis behaved on a wider range of issues. The missionaries, however, did not want to bother about it beyond a point. What they wanted was a congregation of Adivasi faithfuls whose lives they thought they had rescued from heathen beliefs and practices. The congregation of the faithfuls was then expected to look upon the organization of dairying as any other religious undertaking: always needing the guidance of the spiritual leader. The missionaries thus ensured a place for themselves in the lives of the Adivasis, including in cooperative dairying.

And yet from time to time, the inexplicable, in Christian terms, happened. For no 'rationally' explicable reason, the Adivasis behaved, as far as the missionaries were concerned, in strange ways.

Culturally speaking, the Adivasis had their own deeply assimilated norms of social behaviour which then governed their overt conduct. Those norms had their own variety and complexity, and they could not be fully explained or understood in terms of an extraneous belief system.

The Adivasi attitude to death baffled the Jesuit Fathers. They could not understand the loud yells and clapping of hands when the Adivasis saw someone dying in a movie. For the Adivasis, when someone dies, he just leaves. His death is not a matter of unhappiness, but for rejoicing, for he goes where he wanted to go. Adivasis therefore clap their hands when they see someone dying in a movie. For dying and death ensure such a journey.

Nor could the Jesuits understand the Adivasi notion of 'time'. For the Adivasis, 'time' was always there. The notion of time as moments ticking away from your own time-span, in short your lost time or unlived time, did not make much sense to them. For them you do not lose anything by not doing what you did not want to do. For them nothing is lost: you simply live in the moment you actually live in.

Since the future moment does not exist, as of now, it simply does not exist. The future is therefore not there. What is there is the present emerging from the immediate past.

Equally different were Adivasi notions of money, saving for a rainy day, or economic advancement. There is a widespread tendency among them to spend money as soon as it is received. To prolong its use, spread it over a variety of possible uses, or to use it in the future when the need arises, all these are either not a part of the earning and spending experiences of an average Adivasi or merely subscribed to by him in words rather than in deeds. Having lived a precarious existence among forests, rivers and hills for centuries, most of them still have problems relating money to living, let alone comfortable or secure living. Money therefore comes to them as something *extra*, to be used on extraordinary things, impulsively and for the momentary excitement.

At the other extreme not having money, or at any rate not enough of it, is not considered to be a terrible state to be in. When you have something to eat, you eat. The rest of the time you look for it, and wait. It was similar to the psychology of the hunter in the days gone by. The days of prolonged hunger in the past through which an average Adivasi passed prepared him for astonishing spells of endurance. Not having money to buy food makes existence uncomfortable for the Adivasis, that is all, but it does not make life more precarious or unendurable than before.

Money for the average Adivasi is for now, not for the future. The use of money, with the future in mind, is not there. Neither does the future frighten nor its uncertainties scare an Adivasi. For him, he would live in the future when it becomes part of his present, and that will decide what he will or will not have then. Life has to be lived with what turns up moment to moment, day to day.

The prolongation of the use of money, provision for a rainy day, future security, etc., are no doubt attractive notions, but not compelling enough to start exercising an influence on the life of an Adivasi yet.

The Jesuit missionary encounter with the Adivasis of Surat was therefore at a very superficial level. Outwardly the Adivasis went along with the prescriptions and directions laid down by their new spiritual leaders making them often wonder how much of the real change they had been able to bring about in the life of these strange people. The situation was best symbolized by the picture or statue of Jesus Christ which the missionaries insisted the Adivasis keep, exclusively, in their domestic corner of worship, usually the kitchen. The Adivasis, on their part, in their polytheistic mode of belief, welcomed a new face, Jesus, along with many others that they had before. The missionaries insisted on the exclusive presence of Jesus. The Adivasis found a way out. Whenever, the missionaries visited their houses, they just rearranged the pantheon. And after the departure of the visitor, the old polytheistic pantheon reappeared. The missionaries expressed their exasperation at that but could do precious little, at least not with the first generation of proselytized Adivasis.

The Adivasi entry into the milk cooperative, to some extent, forced on them a discipline of work with which they were initially not comfortable. The looking after of the animal meant keeping of time, and doing a variety of chores with clockwork regularity. Then the maintenance and the reproductive cycle of the animal, together with various things to be attended to in that connection, involved the average milch owning Adivasi in future planning.

Such a discipline of work was learnt far more naturally and spontaneously by Adivasis from the vets and their actual demonstration than from the constant advice and prescriptions of the all-knowing, and all-extending, Jesuit missionary. In villages where Jesuit paternalism prevailed, vets experienced a strange dualism of demonstrative authority: their own and that of the spiritual leaders. Often there were moments of awkwardness when the latter strayed into areas about which they knew precious little and vets were too embarrassed to correct them in front of their congregation. Unfortunately, in such moments of dualistic awkwardness, the people who mattered most, i.e. the Adivasis, could say very little. In such villages, the vets, the backbone of the dairy organization, made their visits perfunctory and formal, allowing the spiritual leaders to tend their flock in non-spiritual matters as well. Fortunately for the Adivasis such activities were confined to a handful of villages in the district. In the rest the Adivasis, with all their trial-and-error learning, were making gradual headway by actually involving themselves in the democratic process itself. Even in dairying such villages had begun to do much better, in the long run, than some of the externally supervised communities.

Let us now briefly examine the involvement of social workers in building a cooperative movement in some of the villages of the district. A number of those workers were of Gandhian persuasion and some among them had come under the influence of the ideas of JP. What distinguished the Gandhians from the JPians was the demanding, and sometimes mildly militant attitude, within the broad framework of Gandhian ideology, of the latter. The JPians were also more articulate and given more to open criticism than to endurance. Consequently, they often came in conflict with corrupt Congress politicians in the district and the administrators who served their interests. The JPians, nevertheless, were able to prepare a few rural communities for a high degree of self-involvement in public institutions, including the milk cooperative society. Because of their dedication such communities had won high praise from the organizers of Sumul.

As in the case of Amul, and Kaira district generally, the district of Surat too had a high exposure to the Indian national movement. Some of the most memorable battles against the alien rule were fought on the soil of Surat district, the most memorable among them was the Bardoli Satyagraha. Such an exposure to the ideals of political resistance, and actual involvement in it, had left behind some of the most cherished memories, and also self-assurance. And while the cooperative movement was a non-partisan movement, the competition for power in village, sub-district and district public bodies had assumed a virulent partisan character. The Indira years, particularly, were bad for the JPians. Since JP himself had doggedly opposed Indira Gandhi's imposition of the Emergency, she wanted to wipe out the presence of his followers from all the rural communities of India. Consequently, the JPians, and even mild Gandhians, had suffered from the high-handedness of Congress politicians and administrators who were out to please their political bosses.

Within the district the JPians had put up an effective fight. They had mobilized several rural communities, and had succeeded in effectively involving Adivasis and Harijans in various participatory institutions, including the milk coop, in an effective manner. Some of the social workers there had turned a number of institutions into a network of cooperative societies with a high degree of involvement on the part of the disadvantaged sections of the community.

The main area of Gandhian and JPian social workers was Valod taluka. And the leading light of the movement was the veteran Gandhian social worker called Jugatram Dave. One of the centres of his activity was a village called Vedachi. Dave established the Forest Workers' Cooperative primarily to protect Adivasi forest workers from ruthless exploitation by contractors. Ever since that body came into existence, it undertook contract work in forest clearance and road building, eliminating the middle men.

Dave also established a Gandhian social work training centre in Vedachi. Such a centre produced a leadership which then worked in Valod taluka and helped mobilize the socially and economically backward strata of society. The availability of such a leadership, and its mobilization of various backward communities, was of immense value to Sumul in establishing milk cooperatives in those villages. Valod taluka is heavily populated by Adivasis, and without the availability of social workers, trained by Vedachi, Sumul would have had great difficulty in expanding its organization in that area.

In the winter of 1984, the organizers at Vedachi claimed that in India 42 per cent of the population was below the poverty line, out of which, when you take the figures of Adivasis, nearly 60 per cent were below the poverty line. As opposed to that in Valod taluka, which they called *Vedachi pradesh*, only 25.4 per cent of Adivasis were below the poverty line, and they hoped to bring about a still greater improvement there.

The Vedachi social workers had divided Valod taluka into four areas, with ten villages in each. They then appointed a senior social worker in charge of each area, who was supported by men and women social workers trained by Vedachi. Such workers were out in the field most of the time.

Apart from agriculture and dairying, Vedachi social workers also helped their communities in learning new crafts which could be easily marketed. They also ran a flourishing papadam manufacturing centre.

Since the average social worker was attracted to the ideals of JP, the organization of Vedachi could not escape the wrath of Congressmen, including Indira Gandhi. She then saw to it that Vedachi was deprived of all financial assistance from the state government. But that did not deter Vedachi and its social workers. It further steeled their resolve, made them more dedicated, and less dependent on state funds. Their growing independence made them more critical of Congress policies and rampant corruption in its ranks, which in turn brought in more high-handed measures. One of the villages which had come under the influence of JPian social workers was a village called Anaval. Later on we shall examine in some detail the functioning of its village milk cooperative.

The least acknowledged among the mobilizers of various rural communities, for building milk cooperatives, are the veterinarians, Of all the branches of dairying, they, the vets, serve the most crucial one. Their specialization puts them directly in touch with milch animals and through them their owners. They can gain entry into any village community by talking about animals, and the problems of getting the best returns from them. Consequently, if a veterinarian is outgoing enough, and likes to take an interest in the problems of people, over and above their animals, he can have access to various individuals and groups and their decision-making bodies. Throughout our examination of various rural communities, we found that the vets played a crucial role not only in looking after the animals but also in shaping the dairying community into an effective organizational unit. In most instances, they literally took over the task of building milk cooperatives from the social and political workers, administrators, procurement officers, etc.

In Sumul dairy, however, they went a step further. Given a large component of Adivasi population, which had been cut off from the main stream of social and economic life of the region for centuries, the task before the vets in building milk cooperatives in their communities was a formidable one. And what was more, some of those Adivasi communities had no role model nor economic leaders to follow. Wherever there were economic role models, such as Anavil Brahmins and Patidars, they did not encourage many Adivasis to take to dairying. On the contrary, most of them wanted to ensure, as we have already seen, a cheap source of agricultural labour for themselves. Such a situation of indifference, bordering on economic hostility, left the veterinarians of Sumul to their own resources.

Among other veterinarians of Sumul, the part played by Dr H. A. Ghasia in building a large number of milk cooperatives in Adivasi villages deserves a special mention. He literally transformed a large number of tribal communities into a milk producing peasantry. In such an undertaking he received great moral encouragement from the founding father of Sumul, namely Daskaka, and also from Dr Thakorebhai Patel, the managing director.

Ghasia joined Sumul in 1970 when there were only 13 cooperatives in tribal villages. In the following 16 years he built, almost single-handedly, milk cooperatives in 638 villages bringing their total to 651 in 1986. In the bulk of those villages he did not get any help from social workers. There were not enough social workers to go round the district. Consequently, in most of them he had to start with ground zero.

After giving initial training to a group of Adivasis in dairy management, book-keeping, animal feeding and milking, Ghasia moved on to their endorsing the bye-laws of Sumul.Then within three days of intense association with them, he would ask them to elect their own office-bearers. The follow up on such initial work was then undertaken by Ghasia's colleagues. All along his emphasis was on learning by doing. He believed that there was no short cut to avoiding initial mistakes and once they were taken care of, most Adivasis operated their coop organization with remarkable dedication and efficiency. Since Adivasi villages as a rule are far more cohesive than caste villages, their group effort and group involvement bore results in the shortest possible time.

Moreover, since the gender distance among tribals had been, traditionally, minimal, a large number of women without any exhortation had enrolled themselves as shareholders, become members of executive committees and also chairmen of the coops in some villages.

Finally, since their ethic of repayment of what one owes to others is, relatively speaking, much more strictly adhered to, most Adivasi villages have one hundred per cent recovery of the loans advanced to them by financial institutions.

The arrival of milk cooperatives had economically transformed some of the Adivasi villages. Until his loan was paid off, an average Adivasi was able to take home, with the help of one milch animal, anywhere between Rs3 and 10 per day for a period of seven to eight months in a year. After that it was not uncommon to see the amount rising to Rs7 to 15 per day. As a supplementary income it constituted a great economic blessing. Over the years, a continued resource of this kind, with more than one milch animal, was able to help him to improve his dwelling, agriculture, clothing and standard of living generally.

The Adivasis of the district held Ghasia in high esteem, bordering on veneration. In our several annual field research visits to their villages, from 1979 to 1985, we have seen far too many Adivasi faces from village to village, expressing their deep gratitude to what this self-effacing veterinarian has done for them.

The following table of Sumul's milk collection, from tribal and non-tribal villages, bears testimony to the work done by Ghasia and his colleagues in the district:

TABLE 4 *Milk collections by Sumul*[2]

Year	Milk collection (kg)		No. of village coops	
	Non-tribal area	*Tribal area*	*Non-tribal*	*Tribal*
1979–80	11,214,168 (28.4%)	28,340,337 (71.6%)	24	429
1980–81	10,907,700 (26.8%)	37,524,725.2 (73.2%)	25	471
1981–82	11,081,538 (28.5%)	27,867,771.2 (71.5%)	27	529
1982–83	13,039,659 (29.4%)	31,380,310.7 (70.6%)	27	539
1983–84	11,643,012 (26.4%)	32,377,608 (73.6%)	32	562

SOME RURAL COMMUNITIES

Let us now briefly take into account some of the rural communities of
the district where, by means of a variety of mobilization efforts, milk
cooperatives were established. Such cooperatives bear the distinctive
mark not only of their social composition and leadership, but also the
imprints of the various agents of mobilization.

Anaval

Anaval, with a population close to five thousand (1986), represents a
unique example of a social work oriented leadership building its own
network of cooperative institutions including one for milk. Half of its
population consists of different groups of Adivasis such as Halpatis,
Kodagas, Gond, Dhangars, Kotwalias, etc., and the remaining half
consists of Brahmins, Banias, Patidars, Rajputs, Muslims and
Harijans.

Anaval is considered to be the village from where the Anavil
Brahmins originated, but hardly any Anavil family lives there now.
The story goes that the Anavils of the village were cursed by a
supernatural power. They were specifically asked to leave the village
of their origin and live somewhere else or they would die. Consequently, they prefer to live in other villages, sometimes nearby
villages, but dare not risk their lives and well-being in the one from
which their forefathers came.

In the taluka of Mahuva, where Anaval is located, there has been a
well organized cooperative movement launched by the famous
Gandhian social worker Jugatram Dave and his associates. The
village has also been one of the principal centres of the forest workers
cooperative, officially known as Mahuva Taluka Kamdar Sahakari
Mandal. After organizing the forest workers cooperative, it expanded its cooperative activity in other compartments of economic
life including milk. Unlike other milk cooperatives, therefore, the
one in Anaval is an outgrowth of a wider cooperative movement in
the region. Such a background helps it to minimize economic
conflicts and ethnic tensions within various public bodies in the
region.

Anaval's leadership is drawn from the various ethnic groups which
include Patidars, Rajputs, and Muslims. Then there are the leader
apprentices drawn from the Adivasis. Such a cross-ethnic composi-

tion of its leadership helped it to build one cooperative after another and run them efficiently.

After the forest workers coop, the Anaval leadership established its own consumer coop under the title of Anaval Seva Sahakari Samaj. The next in line was the milk cooperative society which was established in 1972. Since its inception it has consistently maintained an 'A' grade audit rating at the hands of Sumul. It has obtained loans for the poor to buy milch animals, seen to it that almost all those loans are paid off in the shortest possible time, and has turned a large proportion of its Adivasis and Harijans into milk producers.

Being a prosperous market village, Anaval has an inordinately large number of shops and offices. Within them, its resourceful leadership saw a big market for printed stationery. So it established a cooperative printing press under the title of Mahuva Taluka Coope-rative Press. Being a cooperative it gets its clientele not only from the village but also from the entire sub-district. Such an enterprise was then followed up by yet another cooperative and that was for buying seeds, fertilizers and agricultural implements on the one hand, and marketing agricultural products on the other. The organization is known as Anaval Khetipak Kharid-Vechan Sahakari Mandali. Finally, one of its major cooperative undertakings is in the field of polishing rice. It has established a highly successful Cooperative Rice Mill in the village.

Let us now look at the functioning of its milk cooperative society. By 1985–86, half of Anaval's milk cooperative membership consisted of Adivasis. Table 5 shows a sample of income from milk per month which some of the Adivasis received. These random figures, from the same month, suggest that large land owners, or owners of more milch animals, do not necessarily become efficient milk producers. And sometimes milk producers with no land come out with better milk productivity per animal than those who owned a large milk herd.

Over the years the Anaval milk coop had become sensitive to the need to help the poorer section of society to obtain loans for milch animals. Such a change was reflected in the following figures. In 1980–81 it helped obtain 13 loans from the Bank of Baroda, ten of which went to higher income groups and only three to Adivasis. In 1982, 30 loans were obtained from the same bank and all of them went to Adivasis. Again in 1983, 32 loans were obtained from the bank all of which once again went to the Adivasis.

In recent years, Anaval had become a prosperous agricultural and commercial village. Its income from various shops and industrial

TABLE 5　*Incomes from milk per month*[3]

Adivasis: Income from Milk in One Month		
Owner of 4 acres of land:	2 Buffaloes:	Rs596
Owner of 1 acre of land:	1 Buffalo:	Rs317
Owner of 1 acre of land:	1 Buffalo:	Rs283
No land	2 Buffaloes:	Rs66
Owner of 1 acre of land:	1 Buffalo:	Rs90
No land	2 Buffaloes:	Rs612
No land	1 Buffalo:	Rs530
Owner of 1 acre of land:	1 Buffalo:	Rs179
Harijans: Income from Milk in One Month		
Owner of 4 acres of land:	2 Buffaloes:	Rs526
Owner of 1.5 acres of land:	1 Buffalo:	Rs136
Owner of 1.5 acres of land:	1 Buffalo:	Rs161
Owner of 2 acres of land:	1 Buffalo:	Rs45
Muslims: Income from Milk in One Month		
Owner of 25 acres of land:	8 Buffaloes and 5 cows:	Rs528
No land:	2 Buffaloes:	Rs133
Owners of 30 acres of land:	6 Buffaloes:	Rs173
No land:	2 Buffaloes:	Rs190
Higher Castes: Income from Milk in One Month		
Owner of 2.25 acres of land (Rajput):	2 Buffaloes:	Rs659
Owner of 2.5 acres of land (Rajput):	1 Buffalo:	Rs253
Owner of 20 acres of land (Kanbi Patel):	5 Buffaloes and 1 cow:	Rs1666
Owner of 4 acres of land (Brahmin):	1 Buffalo and 3 cows:	Rs83

units was estimated to be Rs1.2m; from sugar cane, rice, vegetables and mangoes Rs1.8m; its income from the wages of forest workers could not be estimated; finally, its income from milk was Rs0.5m. Since half of its members were Adivasis, such an income was considered to be a very vital supplementary income.

The Anaval milk coop was aware of the fact that to be able to help the landless to become milk producers. it must solve the basic problem of fodder for their animals, especially during those months when the landless did not have employment as farm labourers. During the months when they worked on the farms, they were entitled to a *bharo* or a headload of farm-cuttings. Consequently, the Anaval milk coop had made a scheme for converting a part of the village *gauchar* or the common grazing land, which was in a poor shape, into a cooperative fodder farm. In Mehsana and Kaira districts, some, though not all, of those fodder farms had done very well indeed. But Anaval had difficulty in persuading the state government to let it do it.

Since most of the leaders and social workers of Anaval were avowedly JPians, sometimes with JP's pictures prominently displayed in coop offices, they were targeted for disfavour and harassment not only by district Congressmen but also by partisan administrators. But that did not demoralize Anaval JPians. They had known all that before and much worse. They therefore had worked out an elaborate system of helping out the landless with milch animals by selling the farm cuttings whenever available at nominal prices. Some of the leaders were even toying with the idea of buying land and then converting it into a cooperative fodder farm. Finally they had decided to wait and sweat out the duration of partisan decison-making in the district and sub-district bodies.

The poorest of the poor among the Adivasis of Anaval were the Kodagas. Some of them seasonally migrated to the Bombay area, in particular to Vasai and Dahisar, and worked there in the salt-making industry. Since they were migrant labourers, employed for a few months only, they were subject to ruthless exploitation by contractors. The seasonal visits to the Bombay area by Kodagas had given them a false sense of an economic alternative. But visit after visit they had returned to their native Anaval almost empty handed.

Since the Kodagas were nearly five per cent of the village population, the ruling party, which was after their vote, wanted to do them a favour with the help of taxpayers' money by building huts for them rather than think in terms of their continued employment in the local area itself.

The Kodagas were high on the agenda of the leaders of the Anaval milk coop. In the winter of 1985, the leaders of the coop were thinking in terms of building a common cowshed with an average Kodaga household owning a milch animal, feeding it and taking care of it, and all that under the strict supervision of the milk coop. Since the Kodagas were the poorest of the poor in the region, they were entitled to loans and subsidies of all kinds. Moreover, the Anaval milk coop had no hesitation in giving an undertaking for recovering various loans from them. The problem was that of how successful or otherwise such common cowsheds were in other villages. In a village not very far from Anaval called Kamlapur, such a common cowshed was not much of a success. The Anaval leadership, therefore, was inclined to wait a little longer till it could come up with a better alternative. Let us now look at what happened to Kamlapur itself.

Kamlapur

This then brings us to one of the poorest of the poor tribal communities in the district, namely Kamlapur. It is inhabited by a segment of Adivasis called the Kothwalias.Within the tribal hierarchy, the Kothwalias are considered to be the lowest of the low. It is widely believed that other Adivasis would not drink water from a Kothwalia vessel or from anything that is touched by them. This is because the rest of the Adivasis consider the Kothwalia cultural and social standards to be very low indeed.

The traditional occupation of the Kothwalias is that of basket-making. But they could not always make a living doing that. Consequently, quite often they were forced to scavenge for discarded food or even consume the meat of dead animals.

The Kothwalias who lived on the edge of forests were often forced to live on various roots and tubers, some of them highly toxic. These were generally found in the forests. Since they were habituated to eating them, it is said that such an intake did them the least amount of harm. On the other hand, the energy given by those tubers, it was claimed, helped an average Kothwalia to go without food for days at a time.

The conditions of the Kothwalias rapidly declined after the establishment of British rule in India. While they were spread in a number of villages, Kamlapur was almost exclusively inhabited by them. One of the social groups which rapidly rose during the British rule was that of the Parsees. They made a lot of money by means of the sale of liquor and then bought land. Through their land purchasing drive they bought most of the land of Kamlapur, including its *gam tham*, residential area, and pushed its inhabitants literally to a narrow strip of land of about three hundred feet wide by the roadside.

The *gam tham* of any village, through various conquests of India by invaders, was considered to be sacrosanct. The residential area of the village always had a certain sanctity even when territories passed from one ruler to another. But in the case of Kamlapur, it was violated. After independence, the Kothwalias of Kamlapur were given another piece of land away from where their original village was located.

Later on, in 1977, a social work organization called the Manav Seva Trust undertook to teach them new skills in basket-making, papadam rolling, poultrying, dairying and fish farming. Of the latter three, poultrying did exceedingly well. In a relatively short period, the organization started marketing eggs and chicken in various urban centres including Bombay. For some reason the fish farm did not get off the ground at all.

The cooperative dairying in Kamlapur had uneven results. Its own ethnic cohesion had helped it build the organization, under the supervision of Ghasia, in the shortest possible time. The Kothwalias elected a lady to look after it who incidentally was also the chairman of the panchayat. What started interfering with the work of the coop was the high degree of paternalism exercised by the Trust. Such a mode of operation worked well in poultrying but not in dairying. In poultry, the average shareholder was also a wage earner. He worked under the direction of a supervisor, and together they produced impressive results.

But so far as dairying was concerned, the Trust went in for expensive cross-bred cows on behalf of the average Kothwalias, and insisted on keeping them in a common cowshed. After that the average shareholder was supposed to look after the collectively owned herd in a common cowshed. That did not go well with the average Kothwalias who did not know which animal belonged to whom. When the coop started faltering, the Trust called Ghasia. Ghasia maintained that only in very rare cases did the collectively owned cowsheds produce good results, and that dairying produced results only in those situations where individuals took interest and responsibility in getting the best results out of the animals they owned. In dairying animal ownership, care and results went hand in hand. After that, reluctantly, the paternalistic Trust, in the winter of 1985, agreed to let the average Kothwalia have his or her animal tied in the back or the front yard, and see what came of it.

The Kamlapur experiment brought home a very vital point in cooperative undertaking, that is that only through self-involvement does one serve, protect and enhance one's own interests and those of one's community, and that not in all branches of economic activity does paternalism produce results; that even the most backward people are likely to produce results when they are actively involved in what they are doing rather than obeying the prescriptions and commands of those above them; and that they would accept up to a point such directions in those areas of activity which are relatively unfamiliar to them. When they come to know how that works and how it can be organized, they would rather look after it themselves.

The mistake which the Trust had committed was in wanting to replicate the kind of organization which had succeeded in poultrying in the field of the milk cooperative. While the communal poultrying worked, the communal dairying did not. In the latter the wisdom of the classic dictum that everybody's responsibility is nobody's responsibility was brought home. Moreover, the care and maintenance of the animal, as we saw in the case of the Chaudhury women of Mehsana, required a much more personal approach which a communal cowshed could not provide.

The harm which the Trust did in being paternalistic was much more than economic. Under its mindless extension of a big brother approach to different compartments of economic activity, it deprived one of the most backward of rural communities of the opportunity of learning and growing in a human sense, by doing. It also deprived the Kothwalias of growing in their human social and economic capacity to be able, eventually, to look after themselves. Only through such human growth could the Kothwalias have regained their dignity as people, which was at the root of the problem in the first place.

In a sense the approach of the Trust was similar to that of the Jesuit missionaries that we examined earlier. With the best of intentions both these agents of change were creating constraints round a backward people who needed only their initial help in mobilizing and organizing themselves. Once they got their own economic organization going, the newly organized people needed their own space to operate, experiment and grow by doing. Instead both these agents were treating them as wards and as ever-dependent people. Both those agents, therefore, made plans for a permanent need in the lives of the people they were helping rather than, after a time, moving on to other areas and activities where they could serve an equally useful role of initiating others into similar undertakings.

Ghata

The village of Ghata is located about forty-five miles from Surat in Vyara taluka. Its tribal population of about 2000 people (1985) consists of Gamits, Chaudhuries and Kothwalias.

The leading light of the village is an Adivasi youth who, after completing his high school education, worked for the government as a forest ranger for ten years, and then decided to return to his village and help his own people. One of the ways by which he could do this was to start a milk cooperative in Ghata. So in 1978 he started off with a membership of 66, and then by 1984–85 he was able to enroll 424. In the same year the income of the village from milk rose to Rs1.4m.

Ghata milk coop, which came up almost entirely as a result of its own leadership, is considered to be a very progressive organization. its membership was evenly spread between its two major segments, Gamits and Chaudhuries. It could not however succeed in making its Kothwalias join the organization. Nearly one-fourth of its members consisted of women.

In terms of land ownership, the membership of Ghata milk coop had the following composition:

Landless:	152
Marginal Farmers:	67
Small Farmers:	120
Medium and Large Farmers:	85
Total	424

In December 1984, the average income of its members from the sale of milk was Rs490 per month. In the post summer month of August, in 1985, the average income per month was Rs320. What the Ghata milk coop had thus achieved was an average income of Rs10 per day for its members even in the lean season.

Along with its achievement in dairying, its leadership had put an enormous emphasis on the schooling of children. In 1985, it claimed that nearly 75 per cent of its school-going children were attending school regularly. The organizers of the coop also claimed that half of its male membership was literate. But the literacy of its women membership was down to only 15 per cent. The village claimed to have produced two graduates, and ten who had taken their high school education. In the heart of the Adivasi region, its youthful chairman was making use of a Japanese calculator to tabulate figures for us.

While Ghata lacked the orderly atmosphere of Jesuit villages or even Kamlapur, there was nevertheless a spontaneity in its meetings and the usual simultaneous talking, shrieking and laughter. When outsiders visited Ghata, there was much less of a specially prepared show for them. For one thing the village did not have any external disciplinary force to bring that about.

There was, nevertheless, evidence of a very high degree of interest and participation in the deliberations of its public institutions. More people spoke, questioned and disputed what was said than was the case in externally controlled villages. In Ghata, then, there was definite evidence of human growth which had prepared a tribal people to operate and develop their own economic institution such as the milk cooperative.

Vankaner

Vankaner, in Bardoli taluka, is situated about 20 miles from Surat. It is a big village of close to 10,000 people. More than half of its population consists of Halpatis, then there is a large group of Muslims, followed by Patidars, Koli Patels, and then Banias, Harijans and other castes. Because of the availability of water, the village grows sugar cane, bananas, paddy and vegetables. In recent years, the diamond polishing industry has also made headway in the village, with its seven diamond polishing wheels providing lucrative employment to its youths.

The milk cooperative of the village was established in 1972. It was the fruit of the efforts of energetic youths in various economically backward communities such as the Halpatis, Koli Patels and Muslims. The local school teachers and social workers also gave a helping hand in organizing it. By 1985, out of its 2000 households, 750 families had enrolled themselves as its members. During the same year, the milk cooperative reported that nearly 80 per cent of its milk collection came from Halpati families. This was indeed a remarkable achievement.

The older generation of Halpatis recalled that in the past they used to work on the farms of the Patidars for starvation wages of Rs2 per day. Now the situation was different.While the majority of them still worked as agricultural labourers, wages had improved, and the *bharo*, of farm cuttings, was recognized as an essential part of the remuneration. The more the Halpatis became attracted to dairying, the more they insisted on the right to have a *bharo*.

With the help of the *bharo*, and loans for milch animals, some of the Halpatis were able to turn around their economic condition. In

1978 a large number of Halpatis took loans. It took them on average three years to pay them back. During that period, after deduction of the loan instalment and expenses on specially prepared cattlefeed, the average Halpati could get Rs5 per day for a period of seven to eight months from each milch animal.

With such a supplementary income, along with *majoori* (wages) the Halpatis bought more milch animals. In 1985, the Halpatis, on average, came out as the largest owners of buffaloes in the village. In recent years they also started adding high milk yielding cross-bred cows to their milk sheds.

The performance of the Koli Patels and Muslims in dairying was second only to the Halpatis. They too took out loans for milch animals, paid them back in the shortest possible time, and supplemented their agricultural income.

In 1985 all the three communities were going towards cross-bred cows. They all were complaining about the difficulty in obtaining them. If they succeed in it, and retain the same intensity of dairy development as they did in past years, one might see a sea change in economic and social relationships within the community. The political change in the village has already occurred. The following will explain it.

Since the founders of the milk cooperative in the village were the three economically backward communities, i.e. the Halpatis, Koli Patels and Muslims, they have tried very hard to see that it does not become an instrument of the rich. While the Patidars of the village are not kept out of the milk coop, unlike in the village of Ode in Kaira, they are, nevertheless, strictly supervised when they become members of the executive committee. Moreover, since one-third of the committee members have to retire every year, the Patidar advantage in any one year, if that, may be temporary. Because of the history of economic relationships between the Patidars and the rest of the backward communities in the region, such a suspicion on the part of the latter is understandable. The last time the Patidars gained entry into the committee in a big way was in 1982, but then they were outnumbered by the rest. Since then the Halpatis, Koli Patels and Muslims have dominated the institution. For the last three years, from 1983 to 1985, the Halpatis have been in the majority in its executive committee and its chairman too has been from that social background.

In November 1985, during the flush season, the income of the village from the sale of milk during one month was Rs1.35m. That was indeed a staggering amount. By any standard it was a substantial amount for a rural community.

It is indeed difficult to know how many Vankaners there are within the district, probably not very many. In most villages, backward ethnic groups have neither the leadership nor the gumption to challenge the economically powerful within their communities. But what Vankaner points out, however, is that it can be done. And what is more, the residents of Vankaner, in particular the down-trodden Halpatis, did it in less than a generation. Their supplementary income from milk had also improved their bargaining position for agricultural wages. What beats down the drive towards improvement in agricultural wages, however, is the importation of surplus agricultural labour from Maharashtra, the neighbouring state, at an incredibly low wage, with large cuts for its contractors and with huge savings for its employers. In the winter months one sees swarms of agricultural labourers from Maharashtra, literally in rags, going in groups from one work location to another. The local agricultural labour, against such competition, is defenceless. Consequently, it has to moderate, quite often, its own demands for wages. Its only hope then in that respect is dairying. As long as the *bharo* is assured it can make good a part of its economic loss by means of dairying. The question is when would its employers get round to stopping it as a part of the wage. Such an eventuality might give a setback to the increasing penetration of dairying in those segments of population which do not have land to sustain their milch animals.

SOME GENERAL OBSERVATIONS

The ultimate question for all the milk cooperatives is not how far they have been able to bring within their protective cooperative umbrella all the milk producers, but, given the conditions of rural India, how far they have been able to convert the resourceless people into milk producers, and thereby extend the protection of their organization to those who need them the most. In so doing we no doubt prescribe a higher standard of organizational effort to milk cooperatives than to most other institutions functioning in rural India. But since milk cooperatives are some of the very few effective organizations in rural India, and there is so much that they can do over and above what they have already done, such a projection of their possible achievement, therefore, becomes a standard for judging them. All efficient and socially concerned organizations of society are often judged more strictly, and from an unusually higher standard, than are other organizations from which not much is expected. To convert the resourceless into milk producers by making use of the various provisions of public policy, and the money already earmarked for them, also by helping them to choose good animals, and then keeping a watchful eye on the ability of the new producers to keep and breed the animals, are now the new and extending challenges for the milk cooperative organizations of western India.

In the past the dairy organizations did not feel that it was their responsibility to go beyond the *actual* milk producers or rural communities. In fact in terms of their by-laws and organizational purpose the existing milk producers were their sole responsibility. In that respect, in their early phase of development, there used to be agreement with the widely articulated sentiment in rural communities that you cannot do anything for the *sadhan vagar na loko* (people without means). The means in question here are milch animals and the land to sustain them. Over the years, those organizations, either by means of their institutional policy or by the efforts of their individual dairyman operating in rural communities and feeling that he could do more for the poor, have come out with efforts of different kinds to expand the milk producing community by bringing in individuals who were formerly considered to be resourceless.

The record of Sumul, in that respect, was highly commendable in view of the fact that the Adivasis did not have a widespread culture of dairying or even milk consuming. Before Sumul built milk coops in their villages, most of them did not have milch animals worth the name. Sumul thus produced the milk producers themselves first, and then turned them into the backbone of its milk supply.

In transforming the milkless Adivasis into milk producers, Sumul was able to make use of the three very helpful resources. First of all, the availability of financial assistance to the Adivasis by means of subsidy and loans, in various parts of the state, was the starting point. No doubt in a number of cases such loans in various parts of the state did not produce the intended results. Nevertheless, wherever socially concerned vets were involved, together with the Adivasi ethic of repayment, such loans were not only used for legitimate purposes but were also paid back in the shortest possible time. Moreover, the vets of Sumul went out of their way to see that good animals were bought by the Adivasis from Mehsana or Haryana. Second, since most Adivasi villages are either on the edge of forests or have easy access to them, the problem of grazing the animal, especially in the case of the landless, was not a difficult one. With the availability of such a resource, their transition to milk producership was therefore much less difficult. Third, the antecedent social cohesion of Adivasi rural communities, with relatively fewer divisions and factions among them, was indeed very helpful in building an organization based on cooperative lines.

The problems for Sumul, in the case of those communities, were in fact of a different nature. Having been on the margin of Indian social organization since the dawn of Indian civilization, the Adivasis had deeply internalized a notion of their own marginality to whatever was going on around them. They had told themselves, repeatedly, that they were an insignificant people and that they and their welfare did not matter to the wider community. Consequently, their leadership was always self-doubting and not given to demanding or claiming what they understood to be meant for them.

The Adivasi leadership had also convinced itself that when it came to running an organization they would not be the right people to do it, and that someone from the higher caste, with his cleverness, education and experience should be brought in to run it. Consequently, initially it needed some effort and patience on the part of the Sumul organization to put it across to the Adivasis that they were as good as any other in looking after their own cooperative organization. Sumul also had to give them training in book-keeping and in dairy management in general. The leadership also needed initial supervision and encouragement. Once those problems were sorted out, the Adivasis went on to build some of the most efficiently run organizations in the district.

There was an unusual problem in building leadership in Adivasi villages. The Adivasis, ironically, by preserving their social cohesion and also a much greater degree of internal egalitarianism, as opposed to caste villages, made it much more difficult for some of their ambitious and gifted individuals to rise to leadership positions. Their own internal equalizing processes were negativating, as it were, the advantages of some of the extraordinary individuals among them to build their own leadership base. Such advantages were thus being dissolved all the time allowing only a margin of difference to ambitious individuals to stay in a leadership position for a short time.

Moreover, it was only the first generation of Adivasis who had left their social seclusion of centuries and were being incorporated into the wider economic organization of the larger community. Consequently, it was difficult for the Adivasi leadership to start participating in the various participatory processes outside the confines of their own village.The best of them, therefore, did not want to go to sub-district or district level bodies. Politically speaking, given their overwhelming numbers, the control of some of those institutions was well within their reach. But as opposed to that, in the sub-district and district level representative bodies one saw more Patidars and Anavil Brahmins than Adivasis. In that sense the Adivasis had yet to cross the political confines of their own village.

Sumul's operation in different rural communities had different results. In villages which were governed by Anavils and Patidars, it had difficulty in reaching out to the poor, especially the Halpatis, of those communities. But in villages where the organization of the coop dairy had easier access to the poor, even for the Halpatis, as in the case of Vankaner, the performance of Sumul in reaching out to them was positive. Its performance in that respect was about the best in those communities where either the local leadership, no matter of which caste, was interested in opening up such access, as in the case of Anaval village, or in rural communities which were entirely composed of Adivasis and other disadvantaged groups.

We also examined in this section, the lasting influence and imprint left behind on the rural communities by the agents of mobilization and their respective philosophies. While some of those communities were quickly 'reached' or 'brought' into the mainstream of the dairy movement or started working 'efficiently' under external direction, they, in the long run, had paid a very heavy price in terms of their own overall development which can come only through self-involvement.

The problem of reaching out to the poor was thus not only an economic problem but also a social and political, in short, a many-sided, problem. For any economic advantage which cannot be self-engineered, in the sense of secured and protected by means of one's efforts and involvement, will rest on an insecure foundation.

Traditionally speaking, the poor and the very poor of India were locked into social and economic disadvantages by her hierarchical social organization. For centuries they merely appealed to the humanity, liberality and charitableness of their social superiors. The appeal of the poor to those above them was always couched in the language of moral obligation and rewards in the hereafter for helping the poor. Those appeals were not couched in the language of economic and political 'demands'. The constitution of free India and various social policies made institutional and even financial provisions for helping the poor. In some cases lines of affirmative action in favour of the disadvantaged, to socially catch up as it were, were also indicated. But that is where it all stopped. To be able to realize those provisions in practice the disadvantaged needed their own social and political capacity to demand them and ensure getting them. This they did not have, and they could have it only by building their own political capacity and by learning to make their own demands effective. For all this they needed to involve themselves first in the various participatory processes of the newly created economic and political institutions of free India. Consequently, whenever the religious and social do-gooders started working for their causes, instead of taking them along and involving them in the participatory processes, they, to that extent, delayed the genuine development of the poor and the very poor.

In that respect the rural communities of the district which benefited the most were precisely those which received a minimal preparation before they involved *themselves* in operating and running their new economic institutions. The busy vets of Sumul spent at the most three days in an average Adivasi village, telling them the essentials of establishing and running milk cooperatives. For the rest, the individuals of those communities had to learn by means of their own actual involvement, and with the help of the greatest teacher of them all, the trial and error procedure.

Consequently, in terms of an all round reaching out to the poor, the helping hand given by smart individuals with vested interests, politicians pretending to champion their causes, and missionaries with all their good intentions, did not serve the long-term interests of the poor. They merely created an illusion of preparing the poor for building and operating new organizations. In most cases the individuals 'served' by them even became permanently dependent on them. In relation to them the poor added their political defencelessness to the already existing economic helplessness. There was then no short cut to learning to defend one's interests, and the interests of one's community, except by involving oneself in the decisions relating to those interests.

4 Sabar Dairy: a promising milk cooperative

In the winter of 1985, the burgeoning world of Indian dairying was stunned when one of its younger milk cooperatives, for want of processing facilities, said 'no' to the milk sent in by its various village units. Sabar Dairy, located in the district of Sabarkantha, in northeastern Gujarat, refused to accept 100,000 litres of milk, for processing and marketing, from its constituting village cooperatives where it had worked so very assiduously to increase milk productivity. All milk cooperatives have known what is called in their lingo a 'flush' season, whereby the milk delivery of the animal starts climbing up towards the end of the monsoon, reaches its climax in mid January, and then declines in the summer months, and normally they are prepared for it. But in the case of Sabar, the milk production in the district had proved all the earlier projections of growth wrong.

By Sabar's own calculation and future planning, its plant in Himmatnagar was expected to handle a steadily increasing flow of milk in the district till the early 1990s. Such calculations were proved to be far too conservative. Sabar had, in fact, underestimated the response to its own extension work and procurement drive. In the winter of 1984, in less than two decades of existence, it received 350,000 litres of milk. That was very impressive, and it expected the district's milk production to level off at that point. But in the following winter, in 1985, its milk production registered a quantum jump and reached a hefty 450,000 litres.

The dairy officials, after that, were literally in panic. Their own extension work had proved far too successful. And what was worse, some of its milk producers were switching in a big way to the highly productive cross-bred cows. Even in 1985, cow's milk constituted nearly 24 per cent of its total milk collection. The figure might have been higher if it had not turned away what it could not process.

During the period of 'flush', Sabar officials tried desperately hard to persuade big milk producers to exercise restraint and send in less milk to their respective village coops. When that did not work, once a week or, on occasions, twice a week it refused to send in trucks to pick up the milk cans. Before such a drastic policy was acted on, nervous Sabar officials visited various villages and arranged meetings

105

at village and sub-district level. In the meetings everyone seemed 'convinced' and yet at the village collection centres the quantity did not diminish. The reason for that was not hard to find. In recent years, the income from milk had become an integral part of every-body's regular income. While some needed it more than others, there was no way of separating those two categories.

In terms of income groups, the well-off milk producers, with cross-bred cows, suffered more than did those whose milch animals consisted of buffaloes. That is because the latter, with the high fat content in buffalo milk, were able to convert the unwanted milk into *ghee* (purified butter). As opposed to that, cow's milk with a much lower fat content could not produce sufficient *ghee*. They, the latter, therefore screamed the most and even threatened to sell off all the cross-bred cows which earlier they were persuaded to buy.

Looking at the predicament of Sabar, and to a limited extent that of other dairies during the 'flush' season, Dr Kurien at the National Dairy Development Board (NDDB) wondered whether they should not start thinking in terms of crisis management of the phenomenon of 'plenty' in milk.

The glut in milk could have been turned into a scheme of providing a cup of milk to school children in the district of Sabarkantha but the bureaucrats and politicians of Gujarat, with their pig-headedness and unworkable ideas, did not allow the proposal to materialize. Sabar undertook to divert the surplus milk from various village collection points to the local schools. It even volunteered to mix a little bit of sugar, for taste, before serving it to children, in return for which it expected to be paid, Rs0.50 (approximately $0.05) per child. That was roughly the amount Sabar was expected to pay to its milk producers.

On its part the Government of Gujarat insisted on Sabar also supplying snacks to children, along with the milk, for a total of Rs0.70, per child. The average milk coop, which first of all did not want to get into the additional service, considered such a suggestion a money losing proposition.

In the winter of 1985 the proposal, much to the disappointment of everyone concerned, including the children – who, on the rumour network, were assured that the proposal was 'definitely' going to be implemented – were deeply disappointed. Had the proposal been implemented, the chances of its being adopted, on a year-round basis, given the increasing productivity of milk in the district, were very bright indeed. And since the government was committed to spending an increasing amount of money in rural areas, it would have had no difficulty in absorbing a little more generous offer to village milk coops. Such a possibility would have also created a new clientele for the milk producers of the district, and by emulation, for other districts as well. One of the worrisome phenomena in the milk industry of Gujarat is that of its production outstripping the slow growing economic capacity of the consumer to buy it and thereby forcing it to go into the field of milk products and look for markets elsewhere.

BACKGROUND

The milk glut crisis of Sabar dairy suddenly made it an object of attention for dairymen throughout the country. To them everything about the district, which came into existence in 1949, was unfamiliar. The district itself was put together by amalgamating portions of various princely states. Its headquarters is located in a town called Himmatnagar, barely fifty miles from Ahmedabad. The latter always considered the former as a backwater, not worthy of anybody's attention. Most of the former princely states and their underlings did not bother to develop the area either educationally or economically. Even its agriculture was in a shocking state, and naturally the people who suffered the most by such neglect were the poor of the district, in particular, the Adivasis. In relative terms the Adivasis of Sabarkantha were worse off than their fellow tribals in the neighbouring districts of Surat and Panchmahal.

The land of the district is uneven, hilly and infertile. The rainfall in the region is erratic and every year a portion of it experiences drought conditions. Consequently it required a special effort by farmers to level up land, top it with good soil brought from elsewhere, reach distant and often expensive sources of water and then get down to cultivating the land. Such efforts were rarely made either by the farmers or by the Kshatriya aristocracy known as the 'Darbars'.

Even the five small towns of the district, i.e. Himmatnagar, Modasa, Idar, Prantij and Talod, did not register any accelerated pace of commercial or industrial activity. They did not even get round to tapping the rich mineral resource in the district consisting of bauxite, bentonite, china clay, limestone, etc.

Some of the villages within the district which were inhabited by the Chaudhuries, the well-known breeders of animals, produced a lot of milk and milk products such as *ghee* and *mawa* (khoa). Their dairying activity, nevertheless, was seriously undermined in the absence of a well organized milk industry.

The milk producers of the district, whether they marketed milk or milk products, never received a fair deal at the hands of the milk traders. The latter, on the other hand, reaped huge profits by marketing them in large cities such as Bombay and Ahmedabad. Some of the milk producers did toy with the idea of a milk cooperative society, but they could not get very far.

The demand for building a milk cooperative organization for the entire district had to wait till the neighbouring districts of Kaira and Mehsana proved the effectiveness of such a proposition. Moreover, such a proposal also needed a demanding and politically pressuring peasantry. For a long time Sabarkantha did not have such a peasantry.

A potentially demanding peasantry finally came from outside on the eve of Indian independence in 1947. It came from the adjoining districts of Kaira, Baroda and Ahmedabad and also from Kutch in northern Gujarat. It first of all bought huge tracts of land from the local Darbars, at throw-away prices, improved its quality, and started agriculture on it on a commercial basis.

The expatriate peasantry preferred to stay on its own farms rather than in villages where it had bought land. It employed farm labourers and tried to keep out of the cleavages and conflicts within those villages. Its settlements, rivalling the established settlement of the village, were known locally as 'kampas' or 'laats'. The villagers had an ambivalent attitude towards them. On the one hand, the kampawalas were despised for being affluent and derided for being from outside; on the other, the employment given by them to the landless, almost all the year round, was considered to be a great blessing.

There was something strange about those kampawalas. The villagers could never identify the actual owners of those kampas. Those who looked like owners were in fact managers. The real owners rarely showed up. They were merely interested in agricultural income from land, an income on which they did not have to pay income tax. Later on, under one rural development scheme or another, they also got several breaks.

Initially the managers of the kampas did not want to get themselves involved in dairying. This is because they needed buttermilk to give to their farm hands as part of the agricultural wage. Later on,

however, when they saw an additional source of income in dairying,
they started pressuring the local leaders, along with small farmers, for
a full-fledged milk cooperative organization for the district on the
lines of Amul and Dudhsagar.

But in the case of Sabarkantha, there were additional problems. Its
proximity to the metropolis of Ahmedabad, on the one hand, and its
own inability to build a self-sufficient dairy industry, on the other,
created peculiar obstacles for the movement towards a cooperative
organization.

Milk and milk product merchants had already established their
own elaborate network of supply to the huge and lucrative market of
Ahmedabad. They had their own agents, milk collectors and transport facilities to ensure a year round supply of milk. They even had
supervisors to oversee the supply, and monitor any problems or
threats to the flow of milk. Several milk merchants had established
their own jurisdictions for the collection and distribution of milk.
They wanted to eliminate competition as well as friction. In a
concerted fashion they warned, and even threatened, milk producers
against joining the proposed milk coop. Such threats, however, did
not work. The milk producers of the district had the examples of the
highly successful coops of Amul and Dudhsagar literally next door.
Sumul was a little too distant for them.

Earlier the city of Ahmedabad had made several attempts to
amalgamate all its existing milk organizations within one cooperative
framework but had little success. There were powerful milk merchants who dealt with a million litres of milk per day. Then there
were the middlemen of all kinds, together with the truckers, politicians and administrators of different levels of government who had
their own sources of income from the ongoing milk trade with all the
adulterations in it. They all paid lip service to the idea of an
amalgamated milk coop but none of them was genuinely interested
in it.

One of the powerful politicians who assiduously tried to bring
about a milk coop in the city of Ahmedabad was Bhurabhai Patel. He
came from the district of Sabarkantha itself. He decided to dump the
idea of a milk coop in Ahmedabad and start working for one in his
own district. Moreover, while he was one of the many contending
politicians-cum-social workers in Ahmedabad, within his own district
his position was unrivalled. Earlier he had the foresight to establish
the Sabarkantha District Cooperative Milk Producers Union in 1964,
which included a few villages. That meant that he already had an
organizational structure. All that he needed to do now was to expand

it. After leaving Ahmedabad, he started working on the possibility of expanding it to cover the entire district.

The next question was how very great was the milk potential of the district as a whole. While like Mehsana, Sabarkantha too had a large number of *mehsani* buffaloes, most of them, barring those with the Chaudhuries, were not in great shape. Moreover, the Chaudhuries, also known in the district as Chaudhury Patels, did not constitute a large enough ethnic group to be able to become the backbone of the proposed milk coop. And as far as the Adivasis and Kshatriyas, including the Darbars, were concerned, they had a long way to go before they could emerge as effective members of a milk producing community.

Looking at some of the above-mentioned problems, the officials of the NDDB in Anand had remained, initially, unconvinced about the potentiality of a full-fledged milk coop organization for the district of Sabarkantha. In the mid 1960s, the politicians and administrators of the district, fired with the excitement of building a milk coop, started putting pressure on the NDDB. At that time the NDDB itself was a new organization trying to crystallize its own sense of direction and was therefore trying to know more about the milk potential of various regions. Along with Bhurabhai Patel and other politicians, there were now administrators of the calibre of C. C. Desai, the well-known retired ICS officer, lobbying for the milk coop organization for the district.

Finally the NDDB, based on its own findings, reached the conclusion that such an organization would do well in the district. Under the Operation Flood-1 programme, Sabar received financial assistance of Rs1.6m to establish the plant, and Dr Kurien himself visited Himmatnagar to lay its foundation stone.

More than the financial assistance, what the fledgling organization needed was an army of trained personnel. Bhurabhai insisted on well tried out, and dedicated men from Amul. Kurien agreed to let him have five of them who were willing to face the challenge of building yet another dairy organization. They were Babubhai Rabari (dairy technology, production, and now managing director); Dr Haribhai Patel (veterinary services, procurement, and extension); R. S. Seth (engineering); G. D. Memon (dairy technology) and M. J. Bhavsar (quality control).

These five founding fathers of Sabar wanted to replicate the performance of Amul in a district which outwardly had neither an agricultural base nor the animal resources of Kaira. But within less than two decades of existence, in a district with limited human and agricultural resources, they built an organization which had excelled the record of Amul during a corresponding period. The founders of Sabar fondly remembered their experiences of Amul and the wider social values which it inculcated. While Amul moved on to bigger and better things, often diluting its earlier idealism, the personnel trained by it carried with themselves the lasting imprint of its early idealism.

For Sabar the initial problem was that of setting up milk cooperatives in villages adjoining the established dairy districts of Kaira and Mehsana. From there, it was easier to ship milk out to Amul or Dudhsagar while Sabar's own plant was under construction. Then there were coop units inside Ahmedabad district willing to accept milk from Sabarkantha villages.

Sabar's own plant was commissioned in 1974. By that time it had developed a capacity for collecting 90,000 litres of milk, most of which was shipped to the neighbouring coops. The absence of good roads, an adequate transport system and chilling plants proved to be major problems in the rapid development of Sabar. In the absence of the growth of a full-fledged trucking industry in the district, milk cans were transported by means of buses, tractors, bicycles, and camel carts. They were then picked up at various points by vehicles from Sabar.

Apart from the experience of constituting milk cooperatives in the villages of the adjoining districts, what helped Sabar most was the antecedent network of cooperative organizations in various sectors of Sabarkantha's economy.

As Dr Karsandas Soneri, in his comprehensive work on the cooperative movement in the district, has pointed out, such cooperatives included the Agricultural Credit Coop, the Cotton Ginning and Pressing Coops, the Traders and Manufacturers Coops, the Forest Workers Coops, etc.[1] Such a pre-existing network of cooperatives, and above all the cumulative experience in running them, enormously facilitated the formation and operation of another cooperative in the district.

In little over two decades, Sabar was able to pump into the economy of the district, through its sale of milk and milk products, the incredible amount of Rs630.60m.[2] It was able to generate this revenue by selling milk and milk products to both the people in the district and those outside, in particular in Ahmedabad. And what is more, in a short time it was able to persuade its milk producers to switch to cross-bred cows. Sabar's annual report of 1985–86 claimed that nearly 20 per cent of its milk collection consisted of cows' milk.

Within two decades Sabar was able to make its district one of the leading dairy districts of India. It brought within its framework the bulk of the villages in the district and established more than 800 milk cooperatives, more than one-fourth of which were in Adivasi villages. Its health services for the animal and cattlefeed had transformed the quality of the herd in the district. The network of roads in the district also improved and villages, because of donations from various local coops, were able to set up their drinking water tanks and build community halls. Being next door to the sprawling metropolis of Ahmedabad, Sabar, barring a flush season crisis, was assured of a big market. But that was a market outside the district. Its main worry was the sluggish demand for milk, and the low consumer capacity to be able to absorb the cost of it, within the district itself. The economic capability of the people to be able to consume milk was growing at a slower rate than Sabar's own ability to produce it. In August 1986, Sabar, like the other major dairies of Gujarat, was worried about the part of its unsold stock of milk products, particularly of milk powder and *ghee*.

SOME SPECIAL PROBLEMS

Milk cooperatives in India, which are essentially grass-roots organizations, have to take into account, at least initially, the peculiar responses of various ethnic communities to the development stimulus implicit in dairying. Not all of them respond in a uniform manner in the beginning. Later on, however, the peculiar variations within their responses get ironed out and a common behaviour pattern for the whole community emerges.

The sleepy and placid looking district of Sabarkantha displayed some of the most complex patterns of involvement, and rationales for it, in the development process of cooperative dairying. Some of the major ethnic groups within the social organization of the district, such as the Chaudhury Patels, Kshatriyas, Adivasis, Memons and Harijans did not follow a uniform line of involvement in the development opportunities offered by the milk cooperatives which were opening up in close to a thousand rural communities of the district. Not only were the responses to the development stimulus different, they even needed different types of strategies and agents of change to involve them in the development process of cooperative milk dairying. Let us briefly examine what they were.

The Patels or Patidars had moved from different parts of northern India and then settled in Gujarat. Their arrival in the district of Sabarkantha had been relatively more recent. Within the district, because of their recent and continuing internal migrations, or migrations across districts, some of the lines of ethnic demarcation betwen them and their close variants get blurred. Thus their three major segments, i.e., Leva, Kadava, and Unjana or Chaudhuries, claim neither a strict line of demarcation from the others nor a definite superiority.

In Kaira district, for instance, the Leva Patidars would claim superiority over others in no uncertain terms. And within them the Patidars of the six *mota gams* (prestigious villages) will make sure, again in no uncertain terms, that you recognize the fact that they are a cut above the rest of the Patidars. Similarly in Mehsana, the Kadava Patidars would claim superiority over the Chaudhuries, and within the Chaudhuries themselves those of certain villages will claim superiority over the rest.

Because of the relatively recent arrival of the Patidars from different regions, including Kutch, their internal differentiation has so far remained confined to residential and matrimonial segregation. Their feeble subjective claims to hierarchical superiority are blurred in the 'frontier' like situation of the district. With the exception of the Chaudhuries, most Patidars have come here in search of economic prosperity through mining, agriculture, commerce and now dairying. So far, therefore, their emphasis has been on making good economically rather than getting involved in the game of ethnic one-upmanship. Consequently, they are content to be regarded as 'different' rather than superior.

The Chaudhuries, because of their relatively longer settlement in this region, have struck roots and have developed a sense of security and permanence. As opposed to them most of the Patidars are new arrivals, with part of their families left behind in other districts. For such semi-rooted Patidars therefore it was too early to start playing the game of ethnic superiority with those who arrived before them.

The Patidar drive and penetration into the interior of Sabarkantha became possible when the hold of the feudal Darbars on the land of the district started declining. Until then they were content to stay on in talukas such as Prantij and Khedbrahma which border other districts with a larger concentration of their own population. In those two talukas they developed agriculture as well as dairying.

Since Sabarkantha in the pre-independence period had not opened up to the entreprenuerial drive of any group, least of all of one from outside, the economic penetration of the Patidars in areas other than those on the periphery of the district was most difficult. But on the eve of independence, and soon after that, the situation began to change and a massive land purchase movement, headed by the Patidars, got underway. The feudal Darbars were unable to see their economic way through the drastic changes that were taking place during the period of the integration of princely states into the Indian union. Consequently on their part there was a panic selling of land. It was during that period that large tracts of undeveloped agricultural land were bought by the Patidars from Kutch, Kaira, Ahmedabad and Baroda.

The Patidars moved very swiftly into the cultivation of those crops which had the highest return. For them the newly acquired land had only one purpose, namely a high return on investment. Such an attitude helped them to launch agriculture on a commercial basis. The Patidars brought their own managerial skill and innovative outlook to agriculture, and barring the kampas belonging to the Kutch Patidars, who were the most unwilling investors and migrants, those owned by others began to look very prosperous in the shortest possible time. No one is sure how many kampas there are in the district but by a rough estimate their numbers are put down as 200 large kampas and nearly three times that in the category of small kampas. It is also said that there are some kampas which are not even there on the revenue list, but this could not be confirmed from other sources. The kampas, as a rule, employ not only the agricultural labour from the villages but also make available to them *bharo* or agricultural cuttings as a part of the wage that they offer. The widespread availability of *bharo* in fact indirectly helped in the spread of the dairy movement in the district.

So far as the kampawalas were concerned, after their initial resistance to dairying, they too took to it in a big way. What attracted them, as could be expected, was the high return on investment which dairying with cross-bred cows promised.

Despite their explicitly exploitative character, and unmixing social disposition, the kampawalas earned the respect of the other agriculturists as well as of the dairymen in the district. After all they worked hard, levelled the uneven land, reached the difficult and distant sources of water, used better seeds, fertilizers, and techniques of cultivation, and also went in for high yielding cross-bred cows so as to be able to get a good return. Looking at them the smaller farmers, with limited resources, also started emulating the cropping pattern of kampawals. For such farmers the kampawalas became role models to follow, given their own limitations.

From the point of view of the dairymen the improved agriculture in the district, with more employment for the landless labourers, and wages which included *bharo*, was most welcome. The milk organization could now involve them into dairying. In a sense the problem of their being landless was, to some extent, overcome in the villages around the kampas, as their daily wages included a headload of farm cuttings. With the help of such cuttings they could now maintain a milch animal and supplement their income.

As in Mehsana, the main milk producing community of the district consists of the Chaudhuries. The bulk of them are small and medium-scale farmers. They, and in particular their women, have an ever improving hereditary skill in breeding animals. They therefore get a very high level of milk yield from the *mehsani*. The Chaudhuries of the district are thus able to supplement their agricultural income in a big way.

The Chaudhuries, as we shall see later on, had a salutory influence on other ethnic communities wanting to take to dairying. By persuasion and emulation the Adivasis too have learnt the skill of animal keeping. But such an emulation often took place within specific villages, rather than spreading to all other rural communities.

The Kshatriyas of the district, unlike those in Kaira, are Darbar oriented and led. That has been the case for nearly the four decades since independence. Since Sabarkantha was ruled by Darbars of the princely states, no one has yet replaced them, in terms of status and social direction, so far as the Kshatriyas are concerned. The Kshatriyas still need to be told what they should do or should not do by the Darbars whose power and economic strength has long since declined. Even when there are development opportunities around, the average Kshatriya waits for a signal from the defunct Darbar or those near him. Since the Darbars themselves are slow in getting involved in various development processes, they further slow down the process of Kshatriya development. In fact the rate of social change among the Kshatriyas of Sabarkantha is even slower than those castes which are traditionally considered to be well below them. The Patidars, Chaudhuries, Venkars (Harijans) and even Adivasis of certain talukas have responded to development opportunities at a faster rate than did the Kshatriyas.

Such a time lag, and delay, is noticeable in Kshatriyas' joining milk cooperatives and making a good job of it in their respective villages. The bulk of the Kshatriyas are small farmers or marginal farmers and while they are in the dairy industry in a big number, they have yet to develop the necessary skill in building and enhancing the milk-giving capacity of their animals. In certain Adivasi villages, specially where the local population is mixed with the Chaudhuries, as we shall see later on, the former have come out with a stunning record of the utilization of opportunities offered by milk cooperative dairying.

While the Patidars have sent a large number of their people, through the elective machinery, to the Board of Directors of Sabar Dairy, the Kshatriyas have so far (1986) sent only two Darbars. Since the Kshatriyas lack an internal social equality within their ethnic group, every time they end up by electing a Darbar to represent them on public bodies.

Four out of the ten talukas of Sabarkantha are considered to be Adivasi talukas. Sabar started penetrating into them after 1976, nearly ten years after it had established itself in the district. In the last ten years, Sabar has established milk coops in 230 Adivasi villages out of some 360 such villages. Since the Adivasi settlements are spread out in various hamlets and since their milk production capacities are also limited, Sabar often ends up by incurring a lot of cost in collecting a few litres of milk. Moreover, in the summer months, some of their milk coop organizations close down and resume delivery in the monsoon. By 1986, nevertheless, about 25 per cent of Sabar's milk collection came from Adivasi villages.

Then there are Memons (Muslims) who are agriculturists. They are mostly in Idar taluka or in and around the town of Himmatnagar. They too have joined milk cooperatives in large numbers.

In Sabarkantha, the ethnic groups which are engaged in milch animal trade are known as Senava. In terms of ritual hierarchy they are considered to be pretty low. Then there are Rabaris, the traditional keepers of the indigenous cows. Very few among these two groups have joined the milk cooperative societies of their respective villages.

Before the milk cooperative movement came to the district, there were, as Dr Soneri's study pointed out, a number of other cooperatives, and such organizations were most suitable for the Patidar economic drive in the district. In fact they economically prospered through the availability of such structures in the district. The cooperatives took away the major problem of marketing whatever they produced. Moreover, whatever inputs they needed, including credit for their business, the cooperatives made readily available. Consequently, when the dairy industry started developing on cooperative lines, they welcomed it, gave it a grassroots character, and worked within it as their own organization.

At the other extreme there were Adivasis who also welcomed it with great enthusiasm. Since there is much less social distance and hierarchy among the Adivasis of Sabarkantha, the cooperative structure of the new dairy industry ideally suited them.

The Kshatriyas of the district were the least prepared for such an egalitarian structure. Since the prolonged feudal experience under the Darbars had resulted in an internalization of norms of hierarchy, the Kshatriyas of the district expected to be led by their social superiors even within the egalitarian cooperative organisation. They therefore took about the longest to benefit from the new development opportunity provided by milk cooperative dairying.

TECHNOCRATS AND POLITICIANS

All milk cooperatives have a built-in problem of relationship between their techno-managerial staff and the politico-managerial component, in short the technocrats and the politicians. Their relationships, mutual interdependence, personal equations, waxing and waning of influence, etc., as we had seen earlier, is a matter of shifting circumstances. By and large, the politicians assume a relatively more important role in setting up a cooperative organization, in doing the initial mobilization work, voicing concerns from the grassroots up, lobbying the state government on various issues of legislation, and keeping an eye on the policies as they shape inside the board of directors. But such an influence begins to decline, in relative terms, once the organization is set up, mobilization work is taken over by the extension workers or by vets, and most of the broad outlines of policy are laid down. At that stage the differences between the politicians and the technocrats are differences, by and large, of perspective and policy, rarely of substance.

Genuine differences begin to arise when the politicians engage themselves in favouring certain individuals for contracts and use their own influence to secure them. Differences between the two also arise when the politicians, with their connections stretching right up to the state capital, seek to use the vast network of cooperative dairying in the district for electoral purposes and thereby also indicate to their party organization how very important they are to their own area. In fact within those districts where milk cooperative organizations exist, there are no other comparable networks of organization stretching right down to each village.

As competition in democratic politics intensifies, politicians naturally want to gain control of the milk cooperatives and use it, in a subtle and not so subtle manner, to serve their partisan or personal political interests.

Earlier in the first chapter we had referred to the changing relationship between the technocrats and the politicians in the organization of Amul. The organization, as we saw earlier, has become increasingly susceptible to the changing political fortunes of parties in the state of Gujarat. Still its own deeply-rooted tradition of the technocrats reminding the politicians of the dos and don'ts of dairy management has often served it well in moments of crisis. How long those organizations will be able to withstand such a wave of politicization will depend entirely on the ability, fearlessness and dedication of the technocrats. From time to time they will have to put the power-hungry politicians within the framework of constraints by reminding them of democratic propriety, legality and the boomerang effect of short-sighted political interference.

So far as Dudhsagar is concerned, the technocrats and the politicians there have worked remarkably well together. Moreover, the original team, which put the dream of a milk cooperative into practice, with some major changes is still around. They therefore act as joint watchdogs against outside interference.

Sumul too was able to ward off the encroaching hand of the politicians in the affairs of the dairy. The credit for this goes as much to the technocrats as to the politicians. Moreover, its board has been politically far too divided to let any one politician use the organization for partisan purposes.

In that respect, Sabar, the youngest of the four dairy organizations, has been the most vulnerable. While the day-to-day relationships between the technocrats and the politicians are most cordial, the district level politicians leaving a large area of operation and expansion to the technocrats, there is, nevertheless, the encroaching hand of the politicians at the state capital wanting to exercise undue influence on the election of the dairy's top officials. In August 1986, when the time came for the election of chairman of the dairy, it is believed that the then chief minister of the Gujarat government took an extraordinary interest in asking the compliant members of the board who they should elect. Messages from the top went out not only on the political network but also on the administrative. The chief minister thus set a poor example of influence peddling in the election of dairy officials.

Sabar's own technocrats, and even some of the resentful politicians, through no fault of their own, were dragged into a situation which will have a chain reaction. From now on, instead of electing their own chairman, they will have to run to Ahmedabad to find out who the chief minister has in mind. The politicians in the state capital took undue advantage of the relative inexperience of Sabar as an organization. Sabar has yet to build its own tradition of non-interference from outside. Before such a tradition could strike roots, it was seriously undermined in the fall of 1986.

In the later 1950s, Morarji Desai, then in the Congress Party, had played an equally disastrous role in the affairs of a university. He politicized the universities by appointing a defeated politician as a vice-chancellor of one the universities of Gujarat. After that the universities of Gujarat could never come out of such brazen politicization. Equally harmful could be the effect of the politicization of the milk cooperatives by power hungry, and small-minded, politicians.

SOME RURAL COMMUNITIES

Let us now take into account some of the rural communities with different ethnic and economic composition. Some have Kadava Patels, Chaudhuries, Kshatriyas, Harijans, Adivasis and kampa agricultural entrepreneurs. They, as we shall see, have come up with different responses to the development stimulus provided by the organization of the milk cooperative society in the district.

Kadiadara

Kadiadara is a village with a population close to 5000 people. Within the district it is considered to be one of the leading milk villages. It is inhabited by a large number of Chaudhury households. Within the Chaudhury social hierarchy itself, its prestige is considered to be pretty high. Some of the Chaudhury households have even higher social status and have given to themselves the surname of 'Desai'. Some of the Desais of Kadiadara are married to Desai women from the equally prestigious Chaudhury village in the neighbouring district of Mehsana called Kheralu. The presence of a large number of Desais in the village has a rub-off effect on other Chaudhuries. They too consider themselves, a claim which is not always fully recognized, to be an integral part of the Chaudhury aristocracy. Apart from the matrimonial links with Kheralu, which makes Kadiadara one of the prestigious villages in the district, the Chaudhuries want to remain in the forefront of their hierarchy by putting an enormous emphasis on hard work, education, agriculture and dairying.

Out of the total membership of 453 in the Kadiadara milk cooperative in 1986, three-fourths were Chaudhuries. Then there were Kshatriyas, Prajapatis, Muslims, Harijans and Adivasis. The village has put an extraordinary emphasis on education with the result that it is always able to get educated men and women in its public institutions.

The Chaudhuries of Kadiadara are considered to be good agriculturists as well as able animal breeders. Among them, the Desais, with their higher social status, seem to work less hard than the rest. But both segments of the Chaudhuries look to the still higher group than their own, namely the Kadava Patels for social standards. There is thus a process of *patidarization* of the Chaudhuries in matters of education, commerce, travel, women's dress, social expenses, and above all participation in public institutions. Since the Chaudhuries are a close variant of the Patidars in the district, and even use the common surname, Patel, they constantly watch the Patidars for social leads and standards. Consequently, the common drive of the Chaudhuries, towards patidarization, often results in concerted efforts on the part of the two segments of the Chaudhuries. There is much less competition among them for seats in public institutions. They have even worked out some kind of rotation for public office for the Desais and the rest within the Chaudhuries. The dominant group of the

Chaudhuries inside the milk coop, nevertheless, takes great care to see that other ethnic groups, including the Adivasis, are represented on its executive committee.

The Chaudhuries of Kadiadara have gone a step further. From 1972 onwards, the Kadiadara milk cooperative under their leadership was directly involved in helping the economically backward segments to obtain loans and then it would volunteer to collect the instalments on those loans. It also has a good record of repayment of loans. Some of the poor members of the milk coop put it to us this way: "We can get good sleep only when our loans are paid off". During the last ten years, the Kadiadara milk coop helped the banks recover loans by means of instalments from 40 individuals. And what is more, the Chaudhuries, well-known for their understanding of milch animals, personally got involved in ensuring that the poor got the best possible animals.

As a village within the Sabar dairy the rating of Kadiadara is consistently high. In 1981, its income from the sale of milk was Rs1.2m. Then in 1983 it was able to add 60 high milk yielding cross-bred cows, which then brought its income to Rs2.3m. As compared to milk, its agricultural income during the same year was Rs5.5m.

Kubadharol

As opposed to Kadiadara, there was the isolated rural community of Kubadharol, inhabited by Patidars with relatively speaking, much less involvement in helping the socially and economically backward segments of their own community. Not only that, they did not even pay in cash to the various service segments of their community. Instead they paid them in kind. The continuation of such a *jajmani* system, whereby you pay in kind for the services rendered by carpenters, blacksmith, barbers, toilet cleaners, etc., often puts such groups to disadvantage. The absence of monetization of the economy almost always favoured the employers, and not those who offered their services. Often they, the latter, were parked with inferior kind of surplus grains which they had to sell in the open market to be able to buy sugar, edible oil, other grains and vegetables.

For all intents and purposes the public institutions of the village, including the milk coop, were used to serving the interests of the

Patidars. With the exceptions of the Harijans, who continued to get loans for milch animals, because they were targeted for development by outside agencies, the other poor segments of Kubadharol received neither help nor encouragement from the ruling group. Kubadharol, in short, represented a typical instance of how the poor of the village depended as much on outside help as on the community in which they lived. If the community itself did not want to do much, then it was that much harder for the outside agencies to reach them.

Perched at the foot of some of the Aravali hill ranges, Kubadharol had a poor access road, and in both a geographical and social sense it was cut off from its neighbouring communities.

The village had acquired its peculiar name from *cuva* (well) and *Dharol*, a Kshatriya who had founded the village. Together, the two words, with a little change in the first, had given to the village a peculiar name of its own.

Originally it was a Kshatriya village but about five generations ago, a clan of Kadava Patidars, with four lineage groups, had come and settled in the village. In the course of time the new arrivals acquired most of its cultivable land. Unlike most other villages in Gujarat, with their irregular and meandering streets, Kubadharol has a look of a well-planned village with its streets crossing one another at right angles. Most of the Patidar houses there are made of brick.

The Patidars of the village, despite being cut off from other communities, had put great emphasis on the education of their children. Consequently, their young men and women went to high school in Vadali, a biggish village some 10 km from Kubadharol. Such visits of the young outside the village exposed them to influences other than those which their families and community wanted them to have. Such an exposure worried the older generation of Patidars no end.

When Sabar launched a campaign for switching to cross-bred cows in the early 1980s, the Patidars of Kubadharol were quick to respond. By 1984–85, nearly half of their milch animals consisted of cross-bred cows. Within the same year the village milk coop, with a membership of 269, most of them Patidars, earned an income of Rs0.95m.

Such a major switch to cross-bred cows, as the subsequent events proved, was not advisable. In the winter of 1985, when Sabar could not absorb all the milk its village coops collected, Kubadharol suffered the most. Since it was not economic to convert cows' milk into *ghee*, the Patidars of Kubadharol had to sell some of their cows.

In a normal monsoon year, the Patidars of Kubadharol did very well for themselves in agriculture. They had a large number of landless farmers working for them. Their income from agriculture coupled with what they got by selling milk helped them to have a good standard of living for themselves. But they did not want to extend a helping hand to others. In continuing the *jajmani* system, and in showing indifference to the welfare of the poor and the very poor, especially by not encouraging them to get loans from the banks and agreeing to collect the instalments of payment, what the vested interests in Kubadharol were trying to ensure was an assured supply of cheap labour for their agriculture.

The Kubadharol phenomenon thus raised the basic issue for various public bodies, including Sabar, of how to get round the powerful interests of the community which did not want the benefits of development policies to reach others. Until the winter of 1986, none of the development agencies were able to penetrate the barrier erected by the people in power in Kubadharol. The vets and the organizers of Sabar often felt very bad about it, but they were powerless. The poor of Kubadharol thus needed more than the formal provision of development policy or the availability of an institution to help them if only they, the poor, could come to them. Years passed and the poor of Kubadharol could on their own neither approach the various development agencies nor persuade the Patidars of the village to do something for them. What they needed therefore was the organizing hand of a social worker who could mobilize them and pull them out of their low self-esteem and fear of their social superiors and whatever they had to offer them. In their case what was needed then was the building of their capacity to demand, pressure, and take what had been provided for them by various provisions in development policies.

Within the same district, with very nearly similar ethnic groups in power, Kadiadara and Kubadharol presented the two extremes of attitude to the poor. The Chaudhuries of Kadiadara accept their obligation of helping out the poor of their village by making use of the machinery of the village milk coop and the availability of various loans for them. The Patidars of Kubadharol, on the other hand, monopolized all the development opportunities for themselves.

Idar

The town of Idar, with a resident population of close to 12,000, has an extraordinarily prosperous look. It has a flourishing transport industry for carrying people to the holy place of Mota Ambaji, a wooden toy industry, a leather industry, and, more recently, an edible oil cooperative supervised by the National Dairy Development Board.

Its resident population consists of Brahmins, Banias, Rajputs, Kshatriyas, Suthars, Muslims and a large number of Bhambhis (Chamar-Harijans).

Sabar dairy wanted to help Idar's downtrodden population, in particular the Bhambhis, who are classed as Harijans, to supplement their income by means of a milk cooperative in their own neighbourhood. Very soon the proposal ran into difficulty, especially at the hands of the people of other castes. Those opposing castes themselves were not very high in the traditional hierarchy, but in the local situation of Idar, their voice was effective. Of all the people, the opposition to a Bhambhi locality based milk cooperative came from the Rabaris (the traditional keepers of animals), Thakores and Suthars. The protesters maintained that they would not give milk to a Bhambhi locality coop, and therefore there should be a separate one in one of their own ethnic localities. They then selected a locality of Idar called Gambhirpura and put intense pressure on Sabar to let them organize a new one for themselves. Sabar resisted the proposal for a long time, but when the local politicians got involved in it, it had to give up a very valuable principle. The official explanation for relegating this vital principle was that Idar is far too big, which is true, to have only one coop. Hence another one.

The Idar milk coop, started by a caste of animal skinners, the Bhambhis, as could be expected, had a shaky start. When it began in 1979 it had a membership of 75, all of them Bhambhis. Then to the delight and relief of Sabar, it started attracting other castes. By December 1985, in addition to 160 Bhambhis, there were 22 Mansuri (Muslims), six Kshatriyas, eight Bharwads, ten Sagars (vegetable vendors), four Banias, one Patidar and three Brahmins. Thus after a shaky start, the Idar milk cooperative had emerged as a multi-ethnic secular coop as Sabar had hoped it would. The non-Bhambhis, after their initial hesitation, decided to treat the surplus milk in the family cowshed strictly as a business. There were murmurs and protests pressuring Sabar to relocate the coop to another locality, but this time it remained firm. Each day Sabar continued to buy milk from the cooperative in the Bhambhi locality worth Rs900, and the major beneficiaries of such a purchase were the Bhambhis themselves.

The Idar milk coop thus represented yet another dimension of the deeply institutionalized social inequality, disadvantage and prejudice stacked up against the weakest segment of Indian society, i.e. the

Harijans. While the Idar milk coop with an uncertain start had a happy ending, there could be a number of instances where such proposals never got off the ground.

Some Adivasi Villages

Let us now briefly examine some of the rural communities with a large Adivasi population, or exclusively inhabited by them. Out of the nine talukas in the district, there are four which are predominantly Adivasi. They are Bhiloda, Khedbrahma, Vijaynagar and Meghraj.

In the taluka of Khedbrahma, there is a village called Matoda. Half of its population consists of Adivasis and the other half mainly of the Chaudhuries. Roughly the same ethnic proportion is reflected in the membership of the village milk coop.

The Adivasis of Matoda watched the Chaudhuries for a long time breeding their milch animals and supplementing their incomes by the sale of milk. Chaudhury skill in breeding animals and maintaining them had deeply impressed the Adivasis. When Matoda came to have its own milk cooperative, the Adivasis were encouraged to join it. By 1986, out of its total membership of 529, there were 234 Adivasis, and nearly half of them were women. Without any special effort or extension work, their womenfolk had joined the milk cooperative.

The Adivasis of Matoda looked to the industrious and highly skilled breeders of milch animals, i.e. the Chaudhuries, as the models for their own economic advancement.

Among the Adivasis themselves, there were sub-groups of Bubadias, Khers and Gamars. The Bubadias, who were the most numerous, and also industrious, were given to emulating the ways of the Chaudhuries in keeping animals. Consequently the Bubadias also became an internal model for the rest of the Adivasis. Through them the Adivasis were linked, as it were, with the Chaudhuries.

Under the leadership of the Bubadias, who had closely watched the Chaudhuries and had also emulated them, the Adivasis took to dairying and began improving their living standard. The village of Matoda sold milk worth Rs1m to Sabar Dairy in the year 1985, a little less than half of which was supplied by its Adivasi membership.

The Adivasis of Matoda displayed all the visible signs of economic prosperity. Their dress, food, dwellings, beddings, vessels in the kitchen, wall hangings, etc., bore testimony to that. What was more, even their emphasis on education, by way of emulation of the

Chaudhuries, had gone up considerably in recent years. The Adivasi parents claimed that nearly 80 per cent of their children, both boys and girls, regularly went to schools.

The Adivasis of Matoda, who always looked to the Chaudhuries as models, had also deeply internalized the belief that they, the Adivasis, needed the people of higher castes to run public institutions, including the milk coop, efficiently, and that when Adivasis in other villages tried to run them, they had often made a mess of them. By way of an example they had mentioned the name of the next Adivasi village called Chada which, as we shall presently see, consisted entirely of their fellow tribals, and was not doing very well. Consequently they wanted to keep out of any involvement which brought on them the responsibility of self-governance and self-direction. It remains to be seen when exactly would they move away from such conviction and try their hand at self-involvement and governance.

The village of Chada had other groups of Adivasis inhabiting it. They described themselves as Gamars, Pargis, Angaris, etc. In 1970 the Chada Adivasis came to have their own milk cooperative with 70 members. By 1986, its membership rose to 275, and during peak seasons the village milk coop sold milk worth about Rs1,500 per day. That amount declined to nearly half during summer months.

The vets from Sabar Dairy often complained that the villagers of Chada did not always take good care of their animals. Despite a lot of exhortation, they would not bring their animals to select locations for routine health checks and artificial insemination. They expected the animals to go on producing milk without periodic care and pregnancies.

The Chada Adivasis, unlike those in Matoda, did not have a role model in animal keeping before them. The latter watched the Chaudhuries of their village and learnt a lot from them by simply watching them, but that is not how the Chadians saw themselves. They were inclined to put themselves down as an inferior people.

In getting them out of such a self-condemnatory mood, their own leadership was not much help. One of their educated young men, who was put in charge of their consumers' coop, had swindled them to the tune of Rs0.2m. He was then locked up in Idar awaiting trial.

In the meanwhile the poverty-stricken Adivasis of Chada were trying to pick up the pieces of their economic life after such a traumatic experience. The damage to them was more than economic. They had now come to the firm, and even reinforced, conclusion that as Adivasis they were no good at managing public institutions, and that the people of *ujadiat como* or upper caste were needed to look after their institutions. In such a mood, they had already appointed a young Patidar to act as secretary to their milk coop in the hope that they, under his guidance, would be able to avoid further financial mismanagement.

For the Sabar dairy officials then the exercise in reaching out to the Adivasis of Chada, and elsewhere, was to tell them that there was nothing wrong with them as people, and that there were as many cases of embezzlement of public funds where the people of higher castes were involved as those where Adivasis were involved. For the dazed Adivasis, who had believed in the moral and intellectual superiority of the people of the higher castes, it was indeed difficult to believe. On their part, therefore, they did not want to take any more risks by appointing one of their own to public office. They now wanted someone socially 'higher' than themselves with, arguably, a higher code of public conduct than their own.

What had happened to Chada was indeed heart-rending. Unlike the Adivasis of Matoda, those in Chada had poor land and still poorer quality milch animals. On top of that they had now become the laughing stock of the Adivasi villages in the taluka of Khedbrahma. Their economic hurt was thus further compounded by their social disgrace.

As the people of Chada were slowly coming out of the severe drought of the year 1985–86, they were fully aware of what their little income from milk had meant to them during the period of economic hardship. Their careworn faces, moist eyes and tattered clothes made one feel that there has to be a way out for them. Perhaps a resident, and dedicated, social worker could get them going again in a few years' time. And if not in agriculture, because of the poor quality land, at least in dairying they could achieve what the Adivasis of Matoda had achieved. But then where to find such a social worker for them. All they had was the socially concerned milk cooperative of Sabar dairy and its vets. Besides, they had a large number of villages in similar economic condition to look after. The only hope for Chada then was to persuade a vet to *adopt* it as his special village and then pull it out of the economic morass in which it had fallen. In August 1986, the Chadians had very nearly succeeded in pressuring a vet to adopt the village. And now it remains to be seen what came out of those efforts.

Thus, as we saw in this section, for the economic development of the Adivasis even in literally next-door villages, the social composition of those communities made the needed difference. The Matoda Adivasis were exposed to the standard bearers in the arts of dairies, namely the Chaudhuries. And unlike some of the other upper castes,Chaudhuries were keen on on sharing their knowledge and skills with others. For a long time before the arrival of the milk cooperative in Matoda, the Adivasis in the village worked on the farms and cowsheds of the Chaudhuries to supplement their income as labourers. In that sense, before they even owned the milch animals, they had their baptism in the art of animal keeping and breeding at the hands of the masters of the craft in the region. The Chaudhuries involved them in all stages of dairying without realizing that some day their cowhands will become milk producers in their own right.

Finally, when the various provisions in the public policy towards helping the Adivasis were in place, and they took loans and subsidies, the Chaudhuries in Matoda coop agreed to recover the amount by means of instalments when milk was brought to it, and in a short period the Adivasis became owners of milch animals in a big way. The Adivasis of Matoda, looking at their own performance, considered themselves to be in the same league as the Chaudhuries.While they too have a deep respect for the *ujadiat koma*, the upper castes, specially the Chaudhuries, so far as the management of public institutions are concerned, nevertheless, they also believe, as all apprentices do, that some day they too would be able to overtake their own trainers.

As opposed to that the Chada Adivasis were entirely on their own. Since Matoda and Chada are located at a distance of 5 km from each other, there is naturally a lot of social interaction between the two groups of Adivasis, and in a sense the Chada Adivasis have looked down upon the Matoda Adivasis for being too obedient to their Chaudhury masters. But that is as far as their boast of total independence could go. But when it came to the economic performance of the Matoda Adivasis, the Chada Adivasis had to admit they had to cover a lot of ground. Moreover, their own standard of living, and near destitute condition, made their boast of independence sound too hollow.

To conclude this section, we need to take into account the particular stage at which the Adivasi development process is and what can effectively trigger it off. As of *now*, they need some economic models, and directions, to follow. On their own , barring a few exceptions, their performance has not been very impressive. While some of the Adivasi communities of Surat did extremely well when left to themselves, others tend to stagnate.

We therefore return once again to the core issue in this presentation and that is there is a differentiated response to development efforts in different groups, and sometimes even the same or similar ethnic groups respond differently. Such responses force us to think in terms of differentiated social and developmental capacities in different social groups, and of segments within them. Eventually such capacities might iron themselves out into a common denominator capacity, but at this stage of India's rural development effort this central fact cannot be ignored. Such an awareness would stimulate a constant re-evaluation of development strategies and how they actually perform given the extreme diversity of economic, cultural and human situations.

What also cannot be ignored is the fact of what the prolonged presence of the hierarchy-cum-exclusion principle of the caste system has done to different segments of Indian society. Such a system has had a devasting effect on the lower strata of Indian society who, even forty years after Indian independence, do not fully believe that they are partners in the development of her society and economy. They continue to believe that development goals and efforts are only for the *ujadiat koma*. Such a belief is reinforced by the fact that since the dawn of Indian civilization that has been the case. To tell them of their genuine inclusion this time around, and then to transform them into the demanders and takers of what has been earmarked for them, will require different kinds of mobilization efforts among them. Of these cooperative dairying is one of the many possible efforts.

Let us now take into account some of the Adivasi villages which have been influenced by social work organizations which emphasized education of their young men and women. One such organization is known as Adivasi Seva Samiti. Since it is close to the holy place called Shamlaji, it is popularly known as the Shamlaji Ashram.

The Ashram was established in 1947, on the eve of Indian independence, by Gandhian Sarvodaya workers. The leading light of the Ashram since its inception is Narsibhai Bhavsar. Its aim has been to uplift the Harijans and Adivasis by means of education and social development programmes. A number of social workers in the Ashram were, earlier, involved in Mahatma Gandhi's constructive programme in rural communities.

The Ashram has established a number of educational, training (carpentry, smithy, electrical work, etc.), and welfare institutions, but its basic emphasis falls on the education of the young among the Adivasis.

The emphasis on the education and training of the individual has benefited, by and large, the individual much more than the rural community to which he belonged. Its net effect was to build an educated elite within the Adivasis. Such an elite had much less interest in staying on in rural communities, which had invested in their training in the first place. Nor were they interested in mobilizing their own people by means of their own involvement for development. With education and training only the individual elite flourished and not their communities. Such individuals often left their communities and moved to the cities where they were often absorbed in the bureaucracy. Their communities, however, remained where they were.

The same was noticeable in the milk cooperative society of the Adivasi villages around Shamlaji Ashram. The Ashram had educated and trained young Adivasis in those villages. But instead of putting their heart into running some of the public institutions, such as the milk coop, those trained individuals were waiting for their opportunity to move out of their rural communities and move to the urban centres where they could find employment that was in keeping with their education and the new status. Consequently, the performance of most milk cooperatives in Adivasi villages near the Ashram ranged from poor to sub-standard.

The organizers of the Ashram were aware of the problem and had even deeply agonized over it. Of all the social groups in Indian society, the Adivasis could least afford the continual loss of their own trained manpower. Very few of those who had emigrated from the community went back to it to help their people. The teachers at the Ashram had tried what they called the remoulding of character of their pupils and warning them against material temptations, but nothing had worked so far. Education and training by themselves were draining away the communities of their own potential leaders and with them also went the hope for the future. In village after village, the Adivasi communities were neither being mobilized, nor involved nor prepared by their own men and women for participation in protecting and advancing the community's interests. Some trained individuals did come back, but they were either too idealistic or too frustrated to be effective. What was needed was a wider involvement in the development and participatory processes and thereby a growing in their own social and political capacity to be able to protect their interests. Their own trained men and women were not there to help them get involved in such processes. Consequently, the Adivasis of such villages always waited for some social worker to turn up from *outside*, adopt the village, and then lead them on to a better future. The problems of such villages then were further compounded by the nature of the development opportunity which touched only their elites and then deprived those communities of the services of those elites. Under another kind of development strategy which could give incentives to the trained personnel to stay on in their communities, at least for the first few years of their new careers, and then move on if they wished, would have immensely helped those communities. But then the people who planned and executed policies for the development of Adivasi communities had no idea what the *actual* problems were. Nor did they bother to find out what were the actual social consequences of such policies.

At the other extreme of the Adivasis, who as a result of their prolonged exclusion from the mainstream of social life in India, were unable to benefit, on their own, by development opportunities specifically created for them, there were the instances of lone individuals from the upper caste who made the maximum use of the economic opportunities which came their way.

One such individual in the district was a school teacher turned farmer. He is Laxmichand Patel from a village called Navarevas in Idar *taluka*. As a teacher, he was transferred to a school in a valley where a Patidar from Kutch had tried, unsuccessfully, to build a kampa. The Kutchhi Patidar had bought land from a former Darbar for as little as Rs50 per acre. After levelling up the land, he was unsuccessful in striking the sources of water in various wells that he had dug. Out of sheer desperation he put his land on the open market for sale for Rs150 per acre. The impecunious school teacher had his heart set on the land. He therefore borrowed money from his relatives and in-laws and bought a huge chunk of it for Rs50,000. After that he was lucky enough to strike water at the very first strike. That enabled him to borrow an additional amount of Rs70,000, level it up, and start the cultivation of cash crops over his entire estate.

Within less than five years, he was able to get a net income of Rs0.4m a year and then pay off his debt. After that his income started climbing up, especially in view of the fact that he was not required to pay income tax on his agricultural income.

In the meanwhile, he also took to dairying and brought several cross-bred cows and a bull. In August 1986, he had more than 50 cross-bred cows in his cowshed with eight electric fans over them and facilities for showers for his entire herd. His cowshed was named

Gayatri Farm, and it collected on average 500 litres of milk per day. The question then was whether he should send that milk to the village milk coop which did not have a total collection of 100 litres of milk from its entire population or should Sabar send its truck to his farm and make the collection. The dairy officials pointed out that their bye-law required them to follow the former alternative. Laxmichand took them to court. The matter was awaiting judicial decision in 1986; in the meanwhile the court had asked Sabar to continue collecting milk from the farm itself.

Laxmichand Patel, as stated earlier, was just an idealistic and dreamy school teacher when he started. He was as poor as most primary school teachers in India are. But he was enterprising and was willing to explore how he could benefit by various development opportunities. There was nothing in his social background or historical experience which told him that he could not do it. At the age of 45, in 1986, with his school teacher manners intact, he was the wealthiest farmer in the district. And he had achieved all that in a period of less than fifteen years.

As opposed to that the Adivasis had come through the most harrowing social experience of exclusion from the mainstream society and were always treated as either not developed enough or not good enough for any vital economic undertaking. Such a prolonged exclusion had also reacted on their psychology and on their social and political capacity to be able to demand what was rightfully theirs. What they needed at this stage of their development at any rate, was mobilization, organization, and self-involvement in the development and participatory processes to be able to overcome their own deeply internalized notions of inferiority and marginality. They have been on the margin of Indian society for so long that they often believe that they do not matter.

Only when the Adivasis rebuild their own social and political capacity, as individuals and as groups, after a prolonged experience of diminution as a people, and as human beings, imposed by Indian social organizations and other historical experiences, will they be able to emerge as individuals and as groups capable of utilizing what has been provided for them in development policy. But given their devastating historical and social experiences, they need, at least at this stage, dedicated social workers to organize them and involve them in the participatory processes and help them overcome their own sense of isolation and diminution. They still think that they are not good enough as people.

SOME GENERAL OBSERVATIONS

Unlike Amul, Dudhsagar and Sumul, what Sabar had to work with was a newly created district, the agricultural resources and cattle wealth of which were not very great in quality. Consequently, the building of a dairy organization, covering the entire district, was, at least in the beginning, an act of faith in the ability of the various rural communities who inhabited it. By the early 1980s, it was clear that the faith of the founding fathers in the district and its dairying capability were not misplaced.

Unlike the two neighbouring districts of Kaira and Mehsana, with fairly well-established milk-producing communities, Sabar had to create, like Sumul to some extent, its own milk-producing community. Sabar, nevertheless, had the prior experiences of Amul, Dudhsagar, and Sumul to draw upon. Moreover, the various talukas bordering other districts, where cooperative dairying had already developed, had helped Sabar to make an effective beginning. Sabar was also fortunate in having several villages with a large population of the expert breeders of milch animals, namely the Chaudhuries. In villages with a sizeable population of Chaudhuries, the work of establishing a milk coop got going with lightning speed.

Sabar's initial problems were in the field of the transportation of milk from villages where the truckers refused to go. The villagers after that had to rely on several devices so as to take cans of milk to the highways where the truckers agreed to pick them up. In the course of time, as the roads of the district improved, that problem was solved.

Sabar's own staff took up the personal challenge of transforming the milk have-nots, among the villagers, into the milk haves. This meant that they had to associate themselves with those villages and treat them as their own responsibility. That they did with the greatest effectiveness. As some of the veterans of Sabar recalled that whenever they had some free time on their hands, they went to villages which were put within the jurisdiction of certain officials. There they often targeted what they called the *phadiawalas*, meaning the turbaned farmers who were likely to be economically backward and probably without milch animals. These officials then saw to it that such individuals got loans for milch animals and then asked village organizers to help them become milk producers. That practice went on for more than a decade. It transformed village after village by means of the interest and dedication of those officials.

The organizers of Sabar did not have much difficulty in making the Patidars or Chaudhuries members of the milk coop. They did face a lot of problems with the Kshatriyas who always waited for signals from the former Darbars. The Sabar organizers therefore caught hold of Darbars to see that they gained access into Kshatriya communities. By the mid 1980s, the Kshatriyas had taken to dairying in a big way, so much so that the capacity of some of the chilling centres near Kshatriya villages had to be expanded. From among the Kshatriya milk producers, 60 per cent were marginal farmers and the rest were either medium, small-scale or landless farmers.

Sabar's penetration into Adivasi areas, although not as successful as that of Sumul, was, nevertheless, quite encouraging. The Adivasis of Sabarkantha district had known about the worst form of exploitation and backwardness in the regimes of former princes and Darbars that one can imagine. Such experiences had given a great setback to the Adivasi capacity to respond to subsequent development opportunities which came their way. By 1986, nearly 25 per cent of Sabar's milk collection came from its Adivasi villages. Although it was not as impressive as that of Sumul's, nevertheless, Sabar had to work with some added disadvantages specially in the form of experiences of ruthless exploitation of the Adivasis during the princely regimes.

Sabar's performance among the Harijans was less impressive. Although it had succeeded in retaining the Idar cooperative in the Harijan locality, it had to take a severe course of action in tackling the opposition of various ethnic groups when they objected to having Harijans as members of coops. There were instances when Sabar was even forced to close down some village milk coops because they would not allow Harijans to join them. But what Sabar could not do, however, was to make certain that milk coops help improve the lot of their Harijans. Ultimately, much depended on the average village taking up the work of socially broadening the base of its own organization. Even if Harijans were allowed to become members, there was no guarantee that the average village would offer the loan giving agency its services to recover the amount by means of instalments. Moreover, the organizers of the milk coop in the village had to make the Harijans feel that they were as much a part of the organization as any other. Those Harijans who did not want bad blood in the village did not want to press for not only loans but even membership of the milk coop for which the Sabar organizers had put up a fight. The general social backwardness of the district had thus created greater problems for its most disadvantaged group, namely the Harijans. In the summer of 1986, Sabar was confident that by persistently trying it would be able to penetrate the barrier of prejudice before long.

5 The Unreached Poor

The poor in India also belong to the traditional lower castes. The relationship between poverty and caste has been there since the dawn of Indian civilization, and yet in the bulk of our efforts to understand the poor we refuse to consider their economic condition against the background of the traditional society, and their place in the social hierarchy which condemns them not only to social inequality but also to social insignificance. And these, when internalized over a long period of time, have stunted their human and social capacity to fight back on their own. They now need a *human* agency, as we saw in the foregoing pages, to help them retrace their position back to a full humanhood, and from there increasingly to become the demanders and takers of what is rightfully theirs. For such a socially diminished people, the mere provisions of five-year plans and policies are not enough. In a very limited sense, and only by chance, the new economic opportunities of dairying also came packaged with a few individuals who, for reasons of their own, took the initiative to act precisely as those much needed human agencies. And wherever they sought to prepare the poor for their own self-involvement, the results were most impressive. In some of those organizations their involvements became models for others to emulate, whereas in others some of the highly effective policies emerged. Such attempts had uneven results. A high profile dairy like Amul appeared wanting in such efforts, whereas Sumul, because of the highly individualized efforts of a few, came out very well through such a test. The most balanced effort was that of Dudhsagar's which tried to institutionalize individual initiatives by means of constant examples set by the people at the very top. After that almost everyone in the institution, right down the line, was involved, in one way or another, in mobilizing the poor of the district.

The milk cooperatives of western India did not reach all the poor of the district. Nor did they claim to have done so. We took the total number of households in various communities, deducted those which had already become members, and then started checking those that were not reached. The bulk of those non-members, as could be expected, were in the poor localities and in the lower castes. Together they constituted roughly a third of the village population. And their reasons for not being members ranged from the absence of means to statements such as 'We do not know what to do,' 'All those provisions are for the *ujadiat koma* (upper castes),' etc.

In a sense each district presented a different kind of challenge to the problem of reaching out to its own poor. To begin with the social and economic composition of Kaira district was not very helpful in extending the benefits of the new economic organization to the poor of the district. Its landowning community, in particular the Patidars, depended heavily on a steady supply of cheap agricultural labour. Consequently, in villages where there was a sizeable population of Patidars, barring a few enlightened families, they did not show much enthusiasm in helping the poor to obtain loans from financial institutions or even to regularize the giving of *bharo* (farm cuttings) as a part of the wages so that the landless labourers may be able to maintain milch animals and supplement their income. Any improvement in their economic condition was viewed as increasing their bargaining position in asking for higher wages. From their point of view, the more destitute and dependent the landless labourers, the more willing they would be to work on terms which the landowning class offered.

The attitude of the Kaira Patidars, apart from the socially conscious among them, was similar to the Patidars and Anavils of some of the sub-districts of Surat. They too wanted their poor to be a constant source of cheap agricultural labour and nothing else. Consequently, in those subdistricts, both of Kaira and Surat, the performance of their respective milk cooperatives, especially in inducting the poor, was not impressive. However, in other subdistricts, where the poor and tribals did not work for the affluent landowners, it was relatively easier, as we saw in the foregoing pages, to penetrate the poverty curtain as long as some individuals from the organization were determined to do so. We also observed in this connection the remarkable work done by the vets of Surat in bringing the Adivasis of the district within the dairy organization.

Then there was the extraordinarye example of Ode where the relatively poor of a few years ago, when they came in for big time, wanted to block the avenues of development of all those who were economically below them. The Kanbis of Ode, as compared to its Patidars, were the underdogs only a few decades ago. Earlier the latter had tried to stop all the avenues of progress of the former. However, when the Kanbis came in for large chunks of Patidar land, through the new land tenure policy, and established and gained control of the milk cooperative, they did not want the other castes of the village to derive benefit by joining the milk cooperative. Amul on its part initially did not want to get itself involved in an ethnic-cum-economic conflict. Consequently for years dairying remained the preserve of the better off in Ode.

However, the relationship between the rich and the poor, both in Kaira and Surat, was not that simple. As more and more water through irrigation became available to their sub-districts, the better-off needed more farm labourers. And whenever such additional labourers could not be imported from the neighbouring state of Maharastra, not only were the employers forced to give a slightly better wage, but were also forced to include the *bharo* as a part of the nominal wage. The increasing availability of the *bharo* vastly facilitated the work of the dairy organizations in persuading the poor to become members of the milk coop.

Moreover, the Adivasi villages in and around forests, as in the case of some of the sub-districts of Surat, did not have an acute problem of fodder as they could graze their animals in forests or get cuttings therefrom. The vets of Surat – who brought about a double revolution, by transforming the Adivasis into milk producers first, even when they did not have a milk culture, and then by transforming them into a principal source of milk, whereby nearly three-fourths of Sumul's milk collection came from such villages – were able to harness that vital resource in a very effective manner.

Sumul's effort in reaching out to its poor sent yet another signal to the milk producing organizations across the state and that is that the most effective route to Adivasi self-development, as in the case of Dudhsagar, which got women involved in dairying, was through their own self-involvement; that in a sense the lack of economic development was not their only problem, or for that matter of the poor generally; that after a point they should be able to stand on their own feet and be responsible for their own continued development; that in a meaningful sense they had to grow in their own social and political capacity to be able to continue claiming further opportunity for their own development. Such an approach would develop them not only economically but also socially and politically. Without such an all-round development, the process of their advancement would remain highly precarious and externally determined all the time.[1]

In this connection we examined a variety of Adivasi communities where the agents of change, and of mobilization, generally, were different. Each of those agents left behind their own imprints. To bring home this point we examined the social consequences of the paternalistic agents such as the well-meaning Jesuit fathers and the Manav Kalyan Trust, on the one hand, and the work done by roving social workers, resident leaders, and swiftly moving and distantly supervising vets, on the other. The latter, as we saw, came out with a substantial all-round development, much beyond the economic, building the Adivasi social capacity for their own further development by means of a participatory process.

In reaching out to the poor, one of the greatest dangers is to start treating them as wards to be looked after forever, and that is likely to happen in the case of all the well-meaning individuals. Such help after some time ceases to be a condition for continuous development.

The Adivasis of Sabarkantha district demonstrated yet another complex problem. Historically speaking, the Adivasis of the district who lived through centuries of indifference and repression practised by its former princely states were far more impoverished and stunted than their fellow Adivasis in the nearby district of Surat. And they, the former, needed much greater assistance in their development. They learnt much more about dairying from resident role models. Some of them worked in the cattle sheds of the greatest breeders of milch animals in Gujarat, namely the Chaudhuries. After such an apprenticeship it was relatively easier for the Sabar vets to turn them into independent milk producers. But those villages which consisted entirely of an Adivasi population, as we saw in the foregoing pages, gave a poor account of themselves as milk producers in that district.

And what is more, even the spread of education did not help such villages. It merely produced a class of migrants to urban centres leaving such villages to fend for themselves. What ultimately made a little more difference to such villages was a direct approach of 'adoption' by Sabar vets and other officials in the hope that the adoptees themselves, at some stage, would become a model for others.

In reaching out to its poor, Dudhsagar adopted one of the most enlightened approaches. First of all, it refused to be mesmerized by its own productivity figures. Repeatedly its organizers told us, 'We should be judged by what we are able to do for the poor of this district.' Then all the senior officials consisting of the chairman, managing director and the senior vet personally went almost every day to the villages, a routine which they had kept up since the early days of their joining the organization. The senior vet, in particular, felt most restless whenever his lab or office work kept him away from his villages. All those officials were out, and often away from their families, working through odd hours of day and night.

Moreover, Dudhsagar maintained a detailed account of all its villages, complete with the various ethnic groups in them, and especially those social groups that had not become members of their respective milk cooperatives. Those officials did not leave the business of helping the poor to the villagers themselves but repeatedly called meetings in various villages and asked the inhabitants to help them. And they then closely supervized what was coming out of such efforts.

Routinely, they would go through the records of membership and milk productivity of various villages and discuss amongst themselves first what needed doing, and then personally visit those villages to point out what more could be achieved by enrolling more members, especially from among the poor, and actively get involved in helping them to get loans for milch animals.

The senior vet, from time to time, used to prepare a list of the poor from various villages for giving away indigenous cows with cross-bred female calves. That of course needed the concurrence of a special committee but he had no problem there. His very presence in the village, and targetting of the poor, also involved the others in the village. One rarely saw rural indifference to its own poor once made aware of it, in Mehsana, at least not on the same scale, as one saw it in other districts. Some of the rich villages in the district, such as Bapupura, even gave loans to the poor of their villages on their own and charged no interest.

The agriculturally backward district of Mehsana, with poor land and very limited water resources, was thus transformed by Dudhsagar, in less than a quarter of a century, in a variety of ways. It generated enormous liquidity from the sale of milk and milk products, which then led to a change in its agriculture because of the enhanced capacity of the farmers to be able to use water from tube wells, better seeds, fertilizers and pesticide. Moreover, its most efficient programme of veterinary service and constant research for high milk yielding buffaloes and cross-bred cows also radically changed the quality of its milk herd. But more remarkable than that was the concern that the organization, and the individuals working within it, showed towards the poor of the district. In one way or another they felt responsible for them. While the academics argued amongst themselves and ideologues passed all the moral judgements, and the politicians and bureaucrats syphoned off the bulk of the money earmarked for helping the poor, the Dudhsagar technocrats and vets used the resources of their organization to target the poor of the various rural communities and constantly found new ways of reaching out to them.

Earlier we had also seen how Dudhsagar, by means of its various policies, tried to narrow down the gender distance and disadvantage by making women the co-partners in membership, animal ownership, animal insurance, and in the decision-making relating to dairying in general. It is too early to say what the consequences of such efforts in helping out one of the traditionally disadvantaged groups are. What one finds in the rural communities of Mehsana, nevertheless, is a gradually increasing presence of women in matters relating to dairying where none were visible before. Formerly, men spoke on behalf of the entire household. They still are the spokesmen for their womenfolk. Women's views are still expressed through male voices but they are no longer ignored. For women are also present when their husbands speak and often supplement and correct them in public.[2] They are neither ignored nor shut-up as in the past.

In the winter of 1985–86, we sent a note to the organizers of all the four dairies saying that their efforts had not yet penetrated roughly one-third of their rural communities, consisting of traditionally lower and economically backward social groups, and that in the years to come they should principally target those groups for development in 'phase two', as we called it, of their effort. The most enthusiastic response to that note was from Dudhsagar, Sabar and Sumul, in that order, followed by Amul.

The phenomenon of rural poverty – and the attempts to reach out to the rural poor with the help of post-independent India's most efficient agency of rural development, i.e. milk cooperatives – when sought to be understood in any specific area, within the framework of its broader social contexts, as we have tried to do and report in the foregoing pages, turns out to be far more varied and complex than our social sciences theories would have us believe. This is because its roots stretch out into cultural, political, and human sources besides the economic.

But apart from the need to identify non-economic factors relating to poverty, our social sciences dealing with society, polity, and economy, which are based on the urban experiences of a few countries of Western Europe and North America, are themselves not very helpful, and that is because the corpus of theoretical knowledge which they use has in it the accretions of the historical and cultural experiences of those societies where it originally developed. To that extent it is also likely to be insensitive to the peculiar experiences and problems of other societies.[3]

The economic and political differences between the rural and urban communities in the industrialized countries of the West are not as great as they are in emerging countries. Moreover, rural communities are viewed as consisting of potential migrants to urban centres. Since the urban civilization of the west is built by such migrants, it is assumed that everyone, sooner or later, would arrive in cities. And since a self-help attitude of the migrants is very much in evidence in urban centres there, it is also presumed by various branches of the social sciences that it is uniformly so in various communities of all societies. Karl Marx saw the degradation and exploitation of a migrant population leading to militancy and working-class movements for greater social justice in the then industrializing countries of Britain, France and Germany. On either side of the ideological divide in the social sciences, i.e. Marxist or liberal, there is an assumption of homogenization of different groups of people into economic classes and such classes would then generate enough political pressure to bring about change in their own economic condition.

Such a body of knowledge was much less at home with societies where various religious and caste groups, despite migration to urban centres, did not merge into classes. And what is more it found it baffling, and saw fit to ignore such a large percentage of population, unmigrated and locked up in the traditional social organization, based on hierarchy, with different status and privilege for different groups within it. Such a body of knowledge refused to see that the poor, besides being economically deprived, were also accorded the status of lower castes. It also refused to explore the essential link between caste *and* poverty. Much less attention was paid to the fact that the hierarchically ordered traditional society not only kept its poor away from economic opportunity, over and above imposing on them the social indignity of lower castes, but also devastated their will and capacity to be able to escape from them. After nearly 3500 years of poverty and social indignity, the poor in India emerged as a highly diminished people unable to respond effectively to development stimulus which came their way after independence.

Ever since the classical civilization of India established its own social organization based on hierarchy, and the resurgent Hinduism in the post-Buddhist period made such an organization extremely rigid, roughly a third of India's population consisting of the lower castes, untouchables and tribals were made to believe that they were what they were because of their *karma* or past deeds, and that there was no escape for them in this life. The *karmic* rationale, rarely used by the upper castes excepting when someone fell ill or died, was then so deeply internalized by the poor, as an explanation of their being deprived, that any attempt to get them out of it was considered to be futile from the very start. So much so that various development provisions and policies, ostensibly earmarked for them, were treated by them as unreal. They had firmly convinced themselves that they were marginal to the rest of society and that they did not matter. Such a sense of marginality often prevented them from taking seriously the various provisions of policy that were made in a period of planning targetting them for development. Least of all could they become the demanders and takers of the new opportunity which was created for them. As we saw in the foregoing pages, the poor in the rural communities always needed a human intermediary, at least initially, to help them benefit from any development opportunity. And we also saw some of the extraordinary results when a vet or a social worker acted as an intermediary to help them benefit in so far as economic opportunity created by cooperative dairying was concerned.

Such a realization forces us to conclude that there is more to the rural poor than only rural poverty; that in their case we have also to take into account the nature of the social organization, of which they are an integral part, the values that are inculcated in them, and how those in turn orient their responses to economic opportunity. Given those disadvantages, stretching back for centuries, it is pointless to attribute to them a capability for self-help. How could such a capability have come through unscathed from what may be said to be the world's longest surviving unjust social organization, namely the caste system?

Ever since Indian independence educated Indians feel embarrassed to talk about caste. While it does determine a lot of their social life, it is believed by them that it should have no place in India's secular society. Consequently, the only people who continue to take it seriously are anthropologists (because of their emphasis on culture), political scientists (because of their study of votes) and marriage brokers. Since economic science largely developed in the West, where there is ethnicity, class, and race rather than caste, as units of social division, it is taken for granted by a number of its practitioners that it need not be taken seriously elsewhere, and that one can get by ignoring it and taking only class as a unit of social analysis. That is a mistake. While the castes are the givens of the social situation in India, classes have yet to crystallize fully, with their own Indian peculiarities. But in so far as the rural poor are concerned, to ignore their castes, and the peculiar disadvantages their hierarchically ordered social organization has imposed on them, would be tantamount to observing them out of their own actual social contexts.

Gunnar Myrdal in his seminal work on *An Approach to the Asian Drama: Methodological and Theoretical* (1970) warned students of the social sciences against equating developing process of countries of the West with those of South Asia. In his words:

> Conditions in the rich western countries today are such that, broadly speaking, the social matrix is permissive of economic development, or, when not, becomes readily readjusted so as not to place much in the way of obstacles in its path. This is why an analysis in "economic" terms, abstracting from that social matrix, can produce valid and useful results. But that judgement cannot be accurately applied to South Asian conditions. Not only is the social and institutional structure different from the one that has evolved in Western countries, but, more important, the problem of development in South Asia is one calling for induced changes in that social and institutional structure, as it hinders economic development and as it does not change spontaneously, or, to any very large extent, in response to policies restricted to the "economic" sphere.[4]

We also need to identify the peculiarities of poverty in rural India. In his writings on social and economic organizations Max Weber, the distinguished sociologist, had warned that the phenomenon of capitalism is not the same everywhere and that a large number of economic, political and religious forces – consisting of land tenure, sharing the fruits of agricultural labour, industry, mining, crafts, guilds, shop production, increasingly unrestricted commerce, expanded role of money and banking, and growth of the modern state, bureaucracy, rational law, impersonal authority, cities, leadership, all these, together with orientations to economic action as implicit in various belief systems – have influenced it.[5]

Similarly, we need to cultivate a corresponding sensitivity to a pluralistic presence of poverty, which also comes about for a variety of cultural, historical and economic reasons, rather than artificially

homogenize the notion of poverty into one single monolithic block so
as to suit our actuality-insensitive concepts of social sciences.

The segments of the poor, where poverty is sought to be located
and eradicated, are a large number of mutually indifferent, and in
some cases even hostile groups. They stand in a vertical economic
and social relationship with the castes which are either in the middle
or in the higher rungs of traditional society. However, among the
lower castes themselves, which are close to one another within the
social hierarchy, there is the inevitable rivalry for status and competition for employment and material gain. The rural poor thus, despite
their poverty, neither form one homogenous group nor do they
always get together for concerted political action for better wages.
Even when they use the expression 'we, the poor', it is very rare that
they are referring to the entire class of the poor in the community.
The reference is more likely to a lineage or a caste group which
happens to be poor.

The isolation of the poor from one another, because of the highly
segmented nature of the traditional society, is a fact. Such isolation,
together with other factors that we discussed earlier, prevents them
from generating effective political pressure to be able to redress their
economic grievances by themselves. Consequently, even within one
rural community where we can locate its 'poor', what we end up by
locating are groups of unrelated and mutually hostile 'poors'. And
the reasons of poverty in each of the sub-groups of the poor are not
always the same, even when the common denominator in all of them
is economic. The poor, then, as stated earlier, are poor for different
reasons.

Since the poor in India are not *one* single socially homogenous
group, in order to identify them you go through a series of ethnic
groups who are locked up, at a traditional social distance from one
another, in an endless series of disadvantages. They stand at different
distances, like a series of valleys, one behind the other, and you do
not reach them all at once.

From a distance, and through a faulty conceptual perspective, you
might see them as one single group. In effect they are several groups,
poised one after another, subject to constraints and disadvantages of
different degrees imposed on them by their traditional social organization and the network of economic relationships based on it.

Face to face with them you come across some of the most inhuman
and uncaring aspects of the great Indian civilization. You also come
across a heap of human wreckage whose will and capacity to be able

to get out of their economic adversity, and social indignity, is reduced to different degrees of ineffectiveness. When we look at the microcosm of the disadvantaged in various rural communities, closely, we do discover a residue of capability to respond to different kinds of development stimulus provided they are accompanied by socially concerned individuals. And as we saw in several rural communities within the jurisdictions of the four milk cooperatives, whenever their own personnel got involved in reaching out to the poor there was response, no doubt of a varying degree.

The four milk cooperatives that we examined have had a limited degree of success in reaching out to their poor. But the success that they had, however limited, suggests that besides policy, opportunity, and budgetary provisions, they, the poor, would also need people to help them get involved, at least initially, in their own self-development.

In the early years of Indian independence there was a vital debate taking place between Mahatma Gandhi and Nehru, on the one hand, and Nehru and Jayaprakash Narayan (JP), on the other. Gandhi believed that after winning Indian independence, the Congress, which then symbolized the Indian national movement itself, should turn its massive effort inwards, to be able to eradicate the deeply institutionalized inequalities and injustices in Indian society, instead of going for public office. Nehru disagreed. He believed that India's problems were so massive that government agencies too should be partners in such an effort. Later on, JP pointed out to Nehru that his position had become, over the years, one of governmentalism and that India's problems of deeply-rooted inequalities were not going to be solved by means of an army of civil servants. Besides, those who were treated as less than social equals for centuries, and had acquired a diminished perception of themselves, had literally to grow out of them in a genuine sense of the term. And they would not unless they sought their self-development through self-involvement. The Indians grew politically, from their earlier subject status, by means of their involvement in the national movement directed against the alien rule, and now they needed a corresponding movement, ensuring their self-involvement, to fight their own deeply rooted social inequalities.

While such a massive movement never materialized, efforts on a limited scale were no doubt made in different parts of India by different individuals and organisations to pursue different goals. The milk cooperatives of western India are a part of such a series of efforts. They have sought to involve the poor, through a participatory mechanism, not only to help them advance economically but also to grow in their social and political capacity to be able to ensure continued advancement. However limited, given the immensity of India's problems, their effort needs to be recognized.

Notes and References

PREFACE

1. These figures were drawn from the aggregates prepared by Amul, Dudhsagar, Sumul and Sabar by going through the records of landownership of the members of the milk cooperative in each of the villages within their respective jurisdiction. Together they looked at the records of more than 3000 villages.
2. A recent study of Dudhsagar, Sumul and Sabar maintained that 'First, it is safe to say that the bulk of the milk supplies come from small and medium category suppliers. Second, landless labour, small and marginal farmers constitute the dominant segment in membership as well as in the supply of milk. Finally, it is heartening to note that landless labourers are taking up "dairy" as an enterprise and as a primary occupation.' The study also maintained that landless labour constituted 17 per cent of the total milk suppliers. See in this connection *Performance of Integrated Milk Cooperatives* by C. G. Ranade, D. P. Mathur, B. Rangarajan and V. K. Gupta (Ahmedabad: Indian Institute of Management, Centre For Management in Agriculture Monograph series No. 111, 1984. Mimeograph.) p. 174.

   Also see in this connection Manubhai M. Shah, *Integration of District Dairy Cooperatives in Gujarat* (Vallabh Vidyanagar: Sardar Patel University Press, 1977). This is an extremely competent work on various cooperatives in Gujarat.

   There is a considerable body of literature on poverty and we have profited by reading the works of Amaratya Sen, M. Ahluwalia, Bhatty, T. Srinivasan, P. Bardhan, V. M. Dandekar, N. Rath, Keith Griffin, Mahmood Khan and others.

CHAPTER 1

1. See in this connection 'The Techno-Managerial and Politico-Managerial Classes in a Milk Cooperative of India' by A. H. Somjee in *Journal of Asian and African Studies*, XVII 1–2 (1982) pp. 122–134.
2. From *The Story of Amul*, 1989.

3. From a personal communication from Amul.
4. 'Social Structure and Peasant Economy' by Raymond Firth in *Subsistence Agriculture and Economic Development*, edited by Clifton Wharton (Chicago: Aldine Publishing Co. 1969) p. 35.
5. 'Cooperative Dairying and Profiles of Social Change in India' by A. H. Somjee and Geeta Somjee in *Economic Development and Cultural Change*, 1978.
6. Geeta Somjee, *Narrowing the Gender Gap* (London: Macmillan, 1989).
7. Quoted by Samuel P. Huntington and Joan M. Nelson in *No Easy Choice: Political Participation in Developing Countries* (Cambridge, Mass: Harvard University Press, 1976) p. 2.
8. See in this connection 'Social Change in the Nursing Profession in India' by Geeta Somjee in *Images of Nursing* edited by Pat Holden (London: Routledge, forthcoming).
9. In the Chairman's Report to his Board of Directors, Manubhai Patel mentioned that 'More than 50% of population of our district lives below subsistence level and it is difficult to imagine the plight of widows/hapless women with no support from anyone.' With help from various social welfare agencies and its own initiatives, Amul was able to help 105 widows to buy milch animals. See in this connection Amul's *Annual Report and Accounts 1982–83* p. 4.

CHAPTER 2

1. We are grateful to the *Journal of Developing Societies* for kind permission to include portions of our papers 'Dudhsagar Dairy: A Cooperative Miracle in an Arid Land', Vol. II, 1986.
2. From a personal communication from Dudhsagar, 1989.
3. By 1986, Dudhsagar was able to organize 14 fodder farms in the district, and help 1525 widows to obtain loans for milch animals. Ibid. p. 5.
4. From a note prepared by Dudhsagar for us in December 1986.

CHAPTER 3

1. These figures were obtained from Sumul Dairy records.
2. From a note specially prepared for us by Sumul Dairy dated 29–12–1984.

3. These figures were collected at the Anaval Milk cooperative. Also see in this connection Ghanshyam Shah, *Economic Differentiations and Tribal Identity: A Study of Chaudhuries* (Delhi: Ajanta Publications, 1984); Also Ghanshyam Shah and H. R. Chaturvedi, *Gandhian Approach to Rural Development* (Delhi: Ajanta Publications, 1983).

CHAPTER 4

1. See in this connection Dr Karsandas Soneri, *Sabarkantha Jillani Sahakari Pravrutini Stithi Ane Bhavi Vikas* (Himmatnagar: The Sabarkantha Jilla Sahakari Printing Press, 1983).
2. *Sabarkantha Jilla Sahakari Dudh Utpadak Sang Limited: Report and Accounts 1985–86* (Himmatnagar: 1986).

CHAPTER 5

1. See in this connection A. H. Somjee, *Political Capacity in Developing Societies* (London: Macmillan, 1982).
2. Geeta Somjee, *Narrowing the Gender Gap* (London: Macmillan, 1989).
3. A. H. Somjee, *Parallels and Actuals of Political Development* (London: Macmillan, 1986).
4. Gunnar Myrdal, *An Approach to Asian Drama: Methodological and Theoretical* (New York: Vintage Books, 1970) p. 26.
5. Max Weber, *General Economic History* (Glencoe, Illinois: Free Press, 1950) *passim*, pp. 275–313.

Index